Footsteps
of Jesus

Text copyright © Perry Buck 2014
Photographs and maps copyright © Perry Buck 2014
www.perrybuck.com

The author asserts the moral right
to be identified as the author of this work

Published by
The Bible Reading Fellowship
15 The Chambers, Vineyard
Abingdon OX14 3FE
United Kingdom
Tel: +44 (0)1865 319700
Email: enquiries@brf.org.uk
Website: www.brf.org.uk
BRF is a Registered Charity

ISBN 978 0 85746 345 6

First published 2014

10 9 8 7 6 5 4 3 2 1 0

Acknowledgements
Unless otherwise stated, scripture quotations are taken from The Holy Bible,
New International Version (Anglicised edition) copyright © 1979, 1984, 2011 by
Biblica. Used by permission of Hodder & Stoughton Publishers, an Hachette UK
company. All rights reserved. 'NIV' is a registered trademark of Biblica. UK trade-
mark number 1448790.

Cover photo: Old City of Jerusalem at dusk, by Perry Buck

Every effort has been made to trace and contact copyright owners for material
used in this resource. We apologise for any inadvertent omissions or errors, and
would ask those concerned to contact us so that full acknowledgement can be
made in the future.

A catalogue record for this book is available from the British Library

Printed by Gutenberg Press, Tarxien, Malta

Footsteps of Jesus

A pilgrim traveller's guide to the Holy Land

Perry Buck

Acknowledgements

The author would like to thank all those who helped him in the writing of this book, including Fred, Mohanned, Sami, Waleed, Maoz, David, Anna, Katz, Einat, Gili, Sue, Belinda, Neil and Felix in Israel and the West Bank, and Paul, Carolyn, Guy, Trystan, Jason, Naomi and Lisa in the UK. Most of all, thanks to Nel for her love and support and for reading the final manuscript.

Please note that all prices, websites and details of third parties were correct at time of going to press and are subject to change.

Contents

Introduction: in the footsteps of Jesus

As a Christian who loves to travel, I've always felt I was missing out on something. Unlike *Hajj* for Muslims or the compulsion to stand before the Western Wall for Jews, there is no central pilgrimage tradition to help us centre our faith or feed our souls. Sure, we've got Canterbury and Rome and we've got the Holy Land, but how many of us actually go? Who has taken the trouble to step out of their home environment and travel to a completely different part of the world? Why should we even feel we need to?

The majority of Christians never go on pilgrimage, and, of those who do, most tend to stick to a very small part of the Holy Land, namely Jerusalem and Bethlehem. But there is so much more to see, especially in the Galilee region. While the Old City of Jerusalem and the Church of the Nativity in Bethlehem are often busy and sometimes packed out, the rest of Palestine and Israel can feel deserted by fellow travellers.

Thinking of the millions who throng Mecca or the crowds walking down to the Western Wall on *Shabbat* (the Sabbath) really makes me jealous, and always has done. In the past, there has been a strong pilgrimage tradition in the Christian faith (think of the *Camino* to Santiago de Compostela in

Spain or the St Paul Trail through Turkey), but today's world can sometimes push such notions to one side. After all, there is no rule to say we must go to these places, no doctrinal need to visit the actual site of Jesus' birth or the places where he lived, worked and breathed, conducted his ministry and eventually died, and maybe this underlines the universal appeal of Christianity. We don't need to follow strict rules to feel close to our God. We don't need to go to the Holy Land. Yet I still feel that we are missing out, because the wonderful thing is that it's all there and so readily accessible. Within a relatively small and easily navigated part of the world, there is every opportunity to walk in the footsteps of Jesus himself. How amazing to think that you can follow his journey through the lands and towns of the Bible, at your own pace and within your own budget, reflecting on readings and experiences as you go, and feeling connected with the world that bore our earthly Lord!

Whether you travel alone or take an organised tour of the Holy Land, there seems to be no definitive, Gospel-driven guide to help you on your way. Of course there are the major commercial guides, some of them beautifully illustrated, with others firmly aimed at independent travellers, but their content is not written for Christian pilgrims. And while there are some Christian-based guides and certainly some dry tomes going into huge detail about biblical sites and the archaeology or history of this part of the world, it would be much easier to bring it all into one place, either online or in a traditional format. So, wouldn't it be useful if, in a single volume, someone pulled together both the spiritual and biblical significance of visiting the homeland of Jesus with the practical and topical information of a backpacker guide?

That's the purpose of this book and the accompanying

website (www.footstepsofjesus.co.uk): to offer a spiritually fulfilling and practically informed journey, one in which we can retrace our Lord's steps through modern Israel and Palestine, in sympathy with the story of the Gospels, yet with an eye firmly focused on the contemporary setting. This is a single volume that you can take away with you or use at home to plan your journey instead of having to read several books on different aspects of the same topic.

Despite the images we see in the media, Israel and Palestine are safe places to visit, with hugely hospitable people. Although it always pays to be aware of security concerns and of the very real issues surrounding Arab-Israeli history, travelling in this part of the world needn't be stressful. Israel is secure and inexpensive, with a mostly benign climate (except in high summer). There are no huge language or cultural barriers to overcome and the transport and tourist infrastructure is excellent.

The Palestinian Territories can be slightly more challenging to navigate but also slightly more rewarding, as anyone who has wandered the alleyways of Hebron and asked how its current situation can be linked to its past will tell you. At the time of writing (2014), travel around the West Bank for a Westerner, whether organised by yourself or with a guide, is efficient, cheap and safe. In short, there has never been a better time to travel to the Holy Land.

The opportunity to meet ordinary people who will bring to life the history of this land for you is what's most precious about any visit. The joy of engaging with fellow Christians as well as our Muslim and Jewish brothers and sisters should also not be underestimated. Above all, the chance to connect directly with the story of Jesus himself is waiting for those who seek it.

Making the most of this book

These pages focus mainly, although not exclusively, on the Holy Land as described in the Gospels. Of course, other locations (such as Mount Sinai or Hebron) are so important biblically that the book covers them too. Essentially, though, this is a description of the Holy Land as lived in and experienced by Jesus, and it stays focused on the territory now contained within Israel and Palestine, specifically Jerusalem, the Galilee region and the West Bank. There is also a short chapter covering the east bank of the Jordan and Mount Sinai and other key locations in Egypt. With travel to the Gaza Strip currently inadvisable, there is no information in this book about travelling there.

So the Gospels provide the main blueprint, with Luke being a particularly useful source: his Gospel contains the most travelling narratives, with a special focus on the events of the final week of Jesus' life as played out in the streets and alleyways of the Old City of Jerusalem. Matthew is a good teller of stories about Jesus' ministry and life around the Sea of Galilee, his miracles and the reactions of contemporary society. The 'Footsteps' sections of the book allow me to relate some of my own personal experiences and reflections based on a decade of travel to the region.

To help you keep your bearings, this chart will help you to tie up Gospel locations and timescales with places mentioned in the book (see the page numbers given):

The birth of Jesus (Bethlehem)	pp. 87–93
Childhood of Jesus (Nazareth)	pp. 137–44
Aged 30, Jesus begins to travel away from his home town of Nazareth	pp. 162–78
Jesus is baptised by John the Baptist (River Jordan)	p. 170
Jesus is rejected in the synagogue (Nazareth)	p. 136
Jesus calls his disciples (Galilee)	p. 172
Jesus' first miracle (Cana)	pp. 144–46
Jesus teaches in the towns of Galilee	pp. 162–72
Jesus delivers the Sermon on the Mount (Capernaum)	pp. 174–75
Jesus feeds a crowd of 5000 (Tabgha)	pp. 171–72
Jesus raises Lazarus from the dead (Bethany)	pp. 133–34
At the age of 33, Jesus travels to Jerusalem for Passover	p. 39
He is greeted by the citizens of Jerusalem as the 'Messiah' but then causes a disturbance in the temple	pp. 55–57
Jesus has a final meal with his disciples	pp. 41–42
Jesus is arrested in Gethsemane	pp. 37–40
Jesus is interrogated by Pontius Pilate and sentenced to death	p. 37
Jesus is crucified at Calvary	pp. 49–50
His body is placed in a tomb	pp. 50–52
His disciples flee but he appears to them after his death	p. 73
The disciples go out to proclaim the message that Jesus is the Son of God	p. 34

–Chapter 1–

Israel and Palestine

❖ Introduction
❖ Arrival, entry and visas
❖ Security
❖ Getting about
❖ Accommodation
❖ Resources

The
Holy Land

LEBANON

Damascus

SYRIA

The
Mediterranean
Sea

Sour

Kiryat Shmona

Golan
Heights

Rosh HaNikra

Rosh Pina

Akko

Zefat

Capernaum

Nawa

Haifa

Tiberius

Sea of
Galilee

Nazareth

Afula

Megiddo

Irbid

Caesarea

Hadera

Jenin

Jerash

Netanya

Nablus

Herzliya

Qalqilya

Mount Gerizim

Tel Aviv

WEST
BANK

Balqa

JORDAN

Jaffa

Amman

Ashdod

Ramallah

Taybeh

Jericho

Jerusalem

Nebi-Musa

Bethany-beyond
-the-Jordan

Ashkelon

Bethlehem

Qumran

Herodian

The
Dead
Sea

Gaza City

Hebron

GAZA

Masada

Khan Yunes

Arish

Be'er Sheva

Karak

ISRAEL

Cairo

Mitzpe
Ramon

EGYPT

Petra

50 km

20 miles

Mount Sinai

Wadi Rum

Red
Sea

Eilat

Aqaba

Taba

12

Introduction

Israel is small—about the size of Wales—and travelling around is generally quick and inexpensive because of the excellent roads and buses and an improving rail network, which even has a high-speed line between Tel Aviv and Jerusalem under construction. Taxis are usually best avoided as they are expensive: shared yellow taxi vans (*sheruts*) work out much better, especially to and from the airport, or if you need to transport heavy luggage or travel on a Saturday (Sabbath), when other local services will have stopped at sundown.

Taxis become a more viable option in the West Bank, however, where they can help you take in several locations—such as Bethlehem, Shepherds' Fields and Herodian—in a single afternoon or day. In general, getting around the West Bank is slower because the roads are inferior, but nowhere is particularly out of bounds other than the Gaza Strip in the extreme south-west of Israel, on the border with Egypt. Travel there is not recommended and will cause delays and problems for you when you re-enter Israel and again when you try to leave.

Security is a constant issue and crossing between Israel and the West Bank through a checkpoint can be time-consuming. Sometimes it's easier if you've taken a public bus or are part of an organised trip. For the time being, it's unusual for everyone to be herded on and off buses, so getting into the southern West Bank in particular is currently very straightforward by this means. Crossing to and from Ramallah at the Qalandia checkpoint is still taking up to an hour, but this is partly due to the poor roads and the size of the border crossing itself. Using the checkpoints at Jalame, Tulkarem and Qalqilya is usually much faster, making access into the West Bank from Tel Aviv and the Galilee simple.

Patience and understanding of both sides' stances on the issue—and all points of view in between—will help you to realise that crossing the checkpoints is just a fact of life in this part of the world and is less important to us as visitors than it is to the people living on either side of the wall. The security wall that has created a de facto border between Israel and the West Bank has been hugely controversial. While the Palestinians were willing to concede a small amount of land once the Israeli government had passed the law creating the wall, the reality is that it has taken more than six per cent of the West Bank from the Palestinians altogether. Rather than being constructed along much of the pre-1967 green line (the armistice line from the first Arab-Israeli conflict in 1949), the wall on the ground has scooped out huge portions of Palestinian land and created huge buffer zones around Israeli settlements. It has also made access to and around Jerusalem from the West Bank almost impossible.

The wall is seen by many, including the international community, as illegal and an infringement of the human rights of the Palestinians, but recent Israeli governments have seen it as a legitimate and successful security measure, which has made the areas on both sides of the wall safer for ordinary people. Its building was motivated by the aftermath of the first and second Palestinian uprisings, or *intifada* (1995–98 and 2001–2003), when suicide bombings within Israel became a regular occurrence. This cost not only many Israeli lives but also thousands more Palestinian lives as the Israeli Defence Forces (IDF) led military incursions into the West Bank in order to chase down militants and disrupt the *intifada* at its root, in places like Nablus. Israeli public opinion demanded something be done and the government, then led by Ariel Sharon, began building the wall in 2002. Over a decade later, there is no denying that both Israel and the West Bank have become much safer, and most people within Israel (and even some Palestinians) credit the wall for this phenomenon. There have been no suicide bombings on Israeli soil since 2006, and security measures throughout both Israel and Palestine have become increasingly relaxed.

An understanding of the recent history of the land and its people helps here. Knowing something about the creation of the state of Israel in 1948 and the war of independence, the two wars of 1967 and 1973, the two Arab uprisings (the *intifada*), the assassination of Yitzhak Rabin, the failed Oslo peace accords, Palestinian elections in 2005–2006 and the construction of the security wall around the West Bank will give you an essential overview and help to explain the situation. An hour or two invested in reading up on the subject will give you a much better insight into what's going on around you once you're in the country itself.

Most of all, don't be afraid to talk to people once you're there—ordinary Palestinians and ordinary Israelis who will almost always want to engage with you about the current political situation. As outsiders with some vested interest and even responsibility (if you're British) for what has happened there, it's very rewarding to engage with the debate: certainly don't shy away from it. One thing you quickly realise is that on the ground the situation is nowhere near as black and white as the media wish to portray. Neither is anything set in stone. You will find ex-Israeli army officers arguing passionately for the full twin-state solution and the removal of all settlements in order to promote peace, and Palestinians arguing in favour of Israeli incursions into the West Bank because they don't trust their own forces to keep the peace between Muslims and Christians. Of course, this all reminds us that the towns and locations of Jesus' life were turbulent 2000 years ago and remain so today; in that respect, today's troubles give us some insight into the biblical past.

Arrival, entry and visas

Many major airlines fly into Tel Aviv's Ben Gurion airport (TLV). El Al has the most extensive network but other big players into TLV include BA, Air France, Lufthansa, Alitalia, KLM and Swiss. United, American Airlines and Delta are the main US carriers flying transatlantic. EasyJet flies from London Luton and Manchester. The journey from the UK takes around four and a half hours. Some charter flights also go into Eilat on Israel's Red Sea coast: try a travel agent for these flights, or a flight booking website.

Cruise ships operating in the eastern Mediterranean (for example, from Cyprus) often call at Haifa, presenting the opportunity for those on board to enjoy a daytrip to Jerusalem or the Galilee. There are no easy overland routes into Israel, however. Its northern borders (with Syria and Lebanon) are closed to most travellers. The Eilat border crossing with Egypt is the busiest overland crossing point, followed by the three crossings with Jordan on Israel's eastern border. EU passport holders can cross at any of these borders in either direction without prearranged visas but note that an Israeli visa entry or exit stamp in your passport will exclude you from future entry to many Arab or Muslim countries. Israeli immigration officials will (usually) stamp a piece of paper for you instead, if asked.

An Israeli stamp in your passport is not an issue for

destinations such as Morocco or Turkey. Although technically it is a problem for the United Arab Emirates (UAE) and other Gulf states, many EU passport holders visit the Gulf with Israeli passport stamps without ever encountering difficulties. Travelling in the other direction, someone with a lot of Arab stamps in their passport will be asked questions about those visits at the Israeli border. In short, if you think the passport stamp issue will cause you problems, just ask. If in doubt about any of this, check the most recent FCO advice (Foreign and Commonwealth Office at www.fco.gov.uk) or look at what the latest online travellers' forums are saying, such as those on the websites of Lonely Planet (www.lonelyplanet. com) or Trip Advisor (www.tripadvisor.co.uk).

UK, EU and other Western nationals do not require a visa and are allowed a minimum 90-day entry on arrival into Israel, which can be extended from within the country. Note that British and other Western Muslims may find that it takes longer to clear Israeli immigration than for individuals from a non-Muslim background. Anyone can be refused entry unless they provide a detailed travel itinerary along with a detailed family history, and everyone, whatever their background, should have their itinerary (specifically, the name and address of accommodation and wider travel plans) to hand for inspection by the Israeli immigration officials upon landing. These officials *will* ask, and that questioning is likely to be repeated when you leave, so try to make a note of the places where you've stayed.

Travel insurance is highly recommended. No specific inoculations are required for Israel, Egypt or Jordan, but it's always worth ensuring that your tetanus jab is up to date (a booster lasts ten years and is usually combined with diphtheria, whooping cough, polio and Hib). The most common traveller ailments are sunburn and diarrhoea—both easily avoided by being sensible in the sun and only drinking bottled water if you know you have a sensitive stomach. On a hot day in Israel, it's easy to get through at least two litres (four pints) of water, and double that amount or more if you are hiking or cycling. A rule of thumb is that if you're not visiting the toilet every two to three hours, you need to drink more. Tap water is perfectly safe to drink in both Israel and the West Bank.

The Israeli shekel (NIS) has for many years hovered around the GBP £1 = 5 NIS mark, or around US $1 = 3.5 NIS. You should always use local currency in Israel and the West Bank, although many larger businesses, such as travel agents or hotels, will also accept payment in US dollars or (less frequently) Euros, or (less frequently still) pounds sterling. There is a wide choice of ATMs across the territories and local money changers are ubiquitous in Jerusalem. Banks can be found in all towns and cities. Always keep your ID with you (passport or photocard driving licence), since you never know when you may be asked for it.

Footsteps

Arriving at Ben Gurion airport's shining new terminal gives a very modern first impression of one of the oldest sites of continuous human activity in the world.

People have been living, working and organising themselves in this part of the Middle East for at least 80,000 years. Even Ben Gurion airport itself is built on the site of several Roman ruins, including ancient Lod, and the road away from the terminal is filled with signs to towns that may stir your memory of biblical episodes— Ashdod, Lod and Megiddo.

The real prize, however, is 40 minutes to the east of Ben Gurion, as you climb steeply up into the Judean hills and find Jerusalem perched on the top of them like—well, like a bride awaiting her suitor, perhaps (Revelation 21:2). At 600 metres above sea level (over 2000 feet) the winter is much colder in Jerusalem than in the rest of the country, so, if you are visiting between October and March, remember to take a jacket. An early morning arrival and walk straight down to the Wailing Wall as the sun comes up on the Old City can send a tingle down your spine, especially with the accompanying cry of the muezzins and the continuous chiming of church bells.

The truth is that the different communities within Jerusalem and Israel have never enjoyed easy relations with one another, but at least first thing in the morning they seem to be in some kind of harmony. Whether they are walking to the wall or going to pray at the mosque or church, everyone is up and about at the crack of dawn in order to worship the same Abrahamic God. There must be some hope contained in that, surely?

Security

The sight of armed soldiers, police and security guards can be a shock for some, but it quickly becomes commonplace and accepted. Israel is a safe destination, but that security comes at a price. The state is perpetually armed and ready for the next conflict. Youthful conscripts in the IDF seem to make up half of all long-distance bus passengers, especially at week-ends, when your luggage may be moved around in order to accommodate a soldier's loaded Tavor assault rifle or bulging army-green rucksack.

Palestine is no less heavily armed, although there is a strict hierarchy between the IDF, Palestinian Authority forces and local police. As a tourist, you are usually afforded more courtesy than locals and there is no reason to feel less secure here than you would anywhere else in the world. If anything, all sides have a vested interest in looking after tourists, and that can sometimes put you in a privileged position—perhaps allowing you to pass through checkpoints first or without being searched, while locals are queuing up and waiting for papers to be checked. During any time of major unrest, of course, the situation will change: you need to be sensible, keep an eye on the news and talk to other travellers. That way, you are unlikely to be surprised or caught out in an area where you perhaps shouldn't be. Virtually all Israeli and many Palestinian security forces speak English and will usually go out of their way to help you if asked.

Checkpoints are commonplace and it's always best to act calmly and seriously at them. Soldiers and police will usually be courteous and may even strike up a conversation to help break the ice with you. Perhaps ironically, considering the media coverage, Israel and Palestine both enjoy a very low level of crime and, in general, are very safe places for tourists. There have been a number of large-scale military incursions into Gaza and Lebanon in recent years, but Israel itself remains secure. In the Palestinian Territories, there may be an increased risk of petty crime but there is no reason to suggest that tourists are less safe here than in Israel or any other part of the world.

The essential message is that all tourists are welcome and nearly all visits pass off without any hitches. If you have any problems, always approach the local police first and, if you are the victim of a theft, always obtain a police report for your insurance company. If and when things change, it will be wise to adjust travel plans appropriately, but until then relax and enjoy travelling around the country.

Getting about

The national bus company, Egged (www.egged.co.il/Eng), runs an extensive, reliable and cheap network of buses to every town in Israel. There are large long-distance bus stations in Jerusalem and Tel Aviv, from which brand new air-conditioned buses depart regularly for every corner of the country, for between £5 and £15, one way. Apart from the long-distance overnight buses, like those travelling to and from Eilat, it's a turn-up-and-go system, with tickets available from booths next to the bus gates or often from the driver.

The Israeli rail network is also excellent, with the principal line running for 200 miles along the coast from Nahariya in the north, via Akko, Haifa and Tel Aviv, to Ashkelon and Be'er Sheva in the south. Walk-up tickets are available either from counters at manned stations or English-language ticket machines on station platforms. Prices are again very economical, with an Akko–Jerusalem ticket, for example, costing around £15 one way. A deep-tunnel, high-speed line between Ben Gurion and Jerusalem is currently under construction, which, when completed, will whizz passengers from the airport to the central bus station in 20 minutes (see www.rail.co.il/EN).

Domestic flights have limited appeal in such a small country, but they do exist, run primarily by Israir (www.israirairlines.com) from SDE DOV airport (a small domestic terminal in the north of Tel Aviv) to Eilat on the Red Sea coast. Prices start from around £80 return.

Taxis are relatively expensive but will obviously appeal if

time is limited or you have a lot of baggage. Travelling from Ben Gurion airport to the centre of Tel Aviv will cost you around £25, while Ben Gurion to Jerusalem will set you back around £40. Always ask the driver to use the meter (they should anyway but they sometimes 'forget') and try to have a map handy to demonstrate that you know where you are going. Just as in many parts of the world, it's common to find yourself being taken on a magical mystery tour around a town before arriving at your stated destination. If you think this may be happening to you, show the driver your map and ask him to point out where you are. Don't believe that your driver doesn't speak English: the Israeli taxi exam is conducted in English and it's a condition of his licence that he will speak Hebrew, Arabic *and* English. If your driver can't be bothered to converse with you properly while you're still at the taxi rank, simply get out and find another one who can.

As already mentioned, shared taxis (yellow *sherut* vans, which will depart once they are full and usually seat seven to nine people) are much better value, offering the convenience of a drop-off to your door but at a fixed price. Ben Gurion to Tel Aviv is about £6, and to Jerusalem about £10. Remember that *sheruts* also run late at night and on Sabbath, even when other public transport has stopped.

Within the West Bank, regular buses are again cheap and reliable. Distances are short but roads are sometimes heavily congested, so you may spend a fair amount of time in traffic jams. Taxis here become a much more sensible option, especially if there are two or more of you in a group, allowing you some flexibility and the chance to haggle a good deal. Taxi drivers with at least some English will be available on most street corners in Bethlehem, Ramallah, Hebron and Nablus.

Car hire is another attractive and cheap option. It's cheaper to book directly with one of the Israeli car hire companies, either online in advance or in person. The major international players (Hertz, Avis and Budget) are here, but the largest local firm is also recommended. Eldan charges less than £20 per day for a small five-door petrol car, rising to £40 per day for a luxury 4x4 (www.eldan.co.il/en). Note that Israeli hire cars cannot be taken into Palestinian territory, apart from those rented out by Green Peace in Jerusalem (www.greenpeace.co.il). Driving through the West Bank in a car with Israeli plates should not present any difficulties.

Accommodation

Accommodation varies in both quality and price across the Holy Land. In general, Tel Aviv and Jerusalem hotel prices are significantly higher than in the rest of the country. The still-growing tourism base in the West Bank supports only a small number of hotels, which, while offering good value for money, can be a bit spartan. Women travelling alone should always be more cautious: never take ground-floor rooms, for example, and try to keep keys inside door locks. We should all be alert to the fact that incidents of sexual harassment of tourists are uncommon but do take place.

In each chapter of this book, there is a list of luxury (over £100 per night), standard (£40–£100 per night) and budget (under £40 per night) accommodation, including Christian pilgrim hostels and guest houses, most of which are found in Jerusalem's Old City and Bethlehem. The familiar surroundings of a Christian guest house (often simply but comfortably appointed) can offer a welcome contrast to the busy streets outside and will allow for prayerful reflection on the day's experiences and engagement with fellow pilgrims.

When booking any accommodation, it's good to try one of the large internet booking sites first and then compare prices locally. Don't be afraid to haggle if the place you wish to stay in is underbooked. Easter and Christmas are especially busy times, as are Passover and Yom Kippur, but, even with the steady increase in overseas visitors in recent years, there is still an over-supply of accommodation in most of Israel for most of the year, and you should be able to turn this fact to your advantage. Again, the main hotel and travel websites like www.hotels.com, www.trivago.co.uk, www.expedia. co.uk and www.hotwire.com often work out well, or you can check places out in person once you have arrived.

Resources

Only a few individual websites are named in this guide, although there is a wealth of general advice for travelling in Israel and the West Bank on the internet. Sometimes, the best way to access the most up-to-date information will be to consult a search engine. This will not only give you the latest information on things like opening times and costs, but it will ensure that if a location has recently been in the news for any reason, it will come up in your search results, enabling you to keep up to date with events on the ground.

For those who may be unhappy at the prospect of travelling independently or alone, there are plenty of Holy Land tour operators online and many who advertise in the Christian media, with fully guided one-week tours starting at around £1200 per person. Aimed specifically at Christian pilgrims, these tours can work out well, even if they are generally more expensive than organising the same accommodation and transport yourself. An organised tour can be less hassle, but sometimes half the fun of travelling is the planning and making your own arrangements. Conversely, if you wish to have other travellers around you constantly, an organised tour may be best for you. If you know of other like-minded friends, why not organise a tour yourself?

Once in the country, there are plenty of small outfits offering day tours to places such as Masada, the Galilee, Hebron and Bethlehem, which can be booked a couple of days in advance. One of the best and longest-established day-tour operators is Green Olive (www.toursinenglish.com). You could also try www.abrahamtours.com (part of www.abrahamhostels.com). These operators are not only good value but ethical, too: they actively engage in community programmes in all communities.

Only you know what kind of traveller you are and which locations you wish to prioritise, but if you have the time and inclination to make your own arrangements, either before you arrive in Israel and Palestine or once you're there, you will almost certainly save money. You will need at least a week or ten days to explore the region, with a two-week trip offering a more realistic time frame to get you round all the major sites. If you are retired or otherwise have time to spare, a month in the region will amply reward the time invested and enable you to really get under the skin of the places and issues associated with the Holy Land. A month would also allow you plenty of time to see more of the West Bank as well as the more obvious locations of Jerusalem, Bethlehem, Nazareth and the Galilee.

As mentioned, Christmas, Easter and the Jewish holidays are the times of the year when you may struggle to find accommodation, especially in Bethlehem and the Old City of Jerusalem, but booking in advance for these times is the obvious solution. Many people may have been planning a trip to the Holy Land for several years and, if you're a long-term planner, you should be able to use this to your advantage, especially when booking accommodation. Other costs, such as transport or car hire, are less flexible and rarely offer any advance booking incentive: a month or so in advance should still enable you to secure a good deal on car hire, for example. Jewish holidays follow a lunar calendar: the latest dates can be checked at www.reformjudaism.org/jewish-holidays.

Visitor numbers to Mount Sinai are well down since the Arab Spring and ongoing unrest in Egypt, while overseas visitors to Jordan are on the way up. Again, it's perfectly feasible to travel independently in Egypt and Jordan, although some people will prefer the security of booking a package with an established firm such as Thomas Cook. Some good Israeli operators, with their ears to the ground, are www.desertecotours.com and www.mazadatours.com.

Other useful websites include:

- www.goisrael.com
- www.seetheholyland.net
- www.biblewalks.com
- http://st-katherine.net
- http://jordanmagic.com
- www.geographia.com/egypt

Further reading

Martin Gilbert, *Israel: A history* (2nd edn), (Black Swan, 2008).

–Chapter 2–

Jerusalem Old City

❖ Introduction
❖ History
❖ The Easter story
❖ Gethsemane and Mount of Olives
❖ Mount Zion
❖ Via Dolorosa
❖ Golgotha
❖ The Church of the Holy Sepulchre
❖ The Western Wall
❖ Temple Mount and the Dome of the Rock
❖ The Muslim Quarter
❖ City walls
❖ Jaffa Gate and the Citadel
❖ Inbound and outbound travel details
❖ Accommodation in the Old City
❖ Eating, drinking and shopping

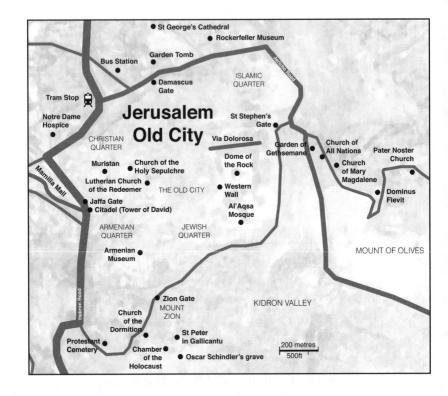

The following labels appear on the map:

- St George's Cathedral
- Rockerfeller Museum
- Garden Tomb
- Bus Station
- Damascus Gate
- ISLAMIC QUARTER
- Tram Stop
- Notre Dame Hospice
- **Jerusalem Old City**
- CHRISTIAN QUARTER
- St Stephen's Gate
- Via Dolorosa
- Garden of Gethsemane
- Church of All Nations
- Pater Noster Church
- Muristan
- Church of the Holy Sepulchre
- Dome of the Rock
- Church of Mary Magdalene
- Lutherian Church of the Redeemer
- THE OLD CITY
- Western Wall
- Dominus Flevit
- Jaffa Gate
- Citadel (Tower of David)
- Al'Aqsa Mosque
- Mamilla Mall
- ARMENIAN QUARTER
- JEWISH QUARTER
- MOUNT OF OLIVES
- Armenian Museum
- Jericho Road
- Zion Gate
- KIDRON VALLEY
- Church of the Dormition
- MOUNT ZION
- Hebron Road
- St Peter in Gallicantu
- Protestant Cemetery
- Chamber of the Holocaust
- Oscar Schindler's grave
- 200 metres / 500ft

Introduction

The city of Jerusalem lives and breathes two things: history and religion. If you accept that the history of humankind has the expression of spirituality at its core, then there is nowhere better equipped to bring this home to us than this once tiny village on the summit of the Judean hills.

So much has happened here that it is hard to know where to begin. As the centre of all three monotheistic faiths, Jerusalem is one of the most fought-over, relevant and endlessly fascinating places on earth. Every corner of every street has a past that the visitor desperately wants to discover, and, in its great monuments to religion, it has more to say to people of faith than anywhere else on earth. This holiness is almost tangible, and, despite the crowds and the touts and the heat, something very special can happen here as you walk around at night or come upon an amazing sight that perhaps you've read or heard about for years. The streets sometimes 'come alive', speaking to us in hushed moments as we turn a corner or kneel before one of the stations of the cross. As one of the city's best historians, Simon Sebag Montefiore, reflects, 'Jerusalem is the place where God meets man.'

Yet Jerusalem also remains at the centre of one of the world's most intractable political problems, and this is the reality that must be understood to get the most out of any visit in person. Both Arab and Israeli sides claim the city as their capital and, while the state of Israel has won the argument for now, it's worth remembering that the city has been in Arab and Muslim hands far longer than it has been in Jewish ones.

All of this comes into sharp relief when you witness the sheer beauty of the city for yourself: for thousands of years, it has been deemed a place worth fighting for. From walking in the morning among the honey-coloured streets of the Jewish quarter, ending up at the Wailing Wall at noon, to standing next to the white-stoned Dome of the Rock or watching a glorious sunset from the Mount of Olives, there is no getting away from the significance of the place and the way it brings all religions involved here to life. If you feel humility and awe inside a great cathedral, imagine that feeling magnified 100-fold as you walk around the basilica of the Holy Sepulchre or pray before the Wailing Wall, the midday sun beating on your back. If Jerusalem is above anything else spiritually, it is also pure theatre, pure drama. You cannot be here without a sense of perpetual awe, a 'wow' constantly waiting to leave your lips. In that respect alone, Jerusalem is a unique place.

Thankfully, the heart of Jerusalem is also a small and easily navigated place, so you will not need to spend day after day walking miles in order to see the most important sights. Split into four quarters—Jewish, Armenian, Christian and Muslim—each part of the Old City has its own definite look and feel. The focus for most people's visits will be among the ancient alleyways, endless souqs and religious monuments. Within even two or three days, though, it's possible to take in the most important sites of the Old City, along with the excellent museums of the New City, all the time enjoying the great food and hospitality spread evenly between the two. So even if you only have a short time to devote to Jerusalem, it will undoubtedly reward you.

History

'The view of Jerusalem is the history of the world; it is more; it is the history of heaven and earth,' said Benjamin Disraeli.

One of the ironies about Jerusalem is that, despite the ancient feel of the Old City, it has been destroyed and rebuilt time and time again, over so many years, that almost none of what we see today corresponds with the city as it was at the time of Jesus. The place we see before us now is old, but not quite biblical in age. The city walls, Temple Mount and other major features date mainly from the Ottoman sultan Suleiman's rule (1520–66), although the retaining walls of Temple Mount are a mix of both Solomon- and Herod-era stone, while the Al-Aqsa mosque dates from around AD1030 and the Dome of the Rock from AD692.

Jerusalem has spent more than a century or two of the past 2000 years lying completely ruined and forgotten. Even 100 years ago, the city held only the tiny remnants of a Jewish population within a half-ruined Old City and among an overwhelming Ottoman-ruled Muslim majority, all packed in behind the city walls we see today. There was absolutely nothing on the surrounding hills except shepherds and their sheep. The fact that the city is now Israel's capital, with half a million Jewish inhabitants, is testament to the force of Israeli political will and the expansion of the city, far beyond its original boundaries, over the past 75 years.

Fabled as the location where Abraham prepared to sacrifice his son Isaac before God, the city was first settled by the Davidian tribes more than 3000 years ago. These people took over the city from the Jebusites and Canaanites who had started a pagan settlement a few hundred years before, on the site of a spring that flowed east towards the rising sun. Jerusalem quickly became an important trading post on the top of the Judean hills, attracting merchants as well as farmers keen to sell their sheep. With desert and windswept pastureland for miles around, the town became a popular place not just to bring cattle to market, but also to escape the worst of the Middle Eastern summer and winter. In such a tough and inhospitable environment, the city became a centre where God spoke to his people about how they could survive their harsh setting.

Crucially, this small trading post attracted the attention of King David, who turned Jerusalem into his Jewish capital around 1000BC. The early city grew around its new religion and the First Temple was constructed by David's son, Solomon, around 965BC. After Jerusalem was sacked by the Babylonians in 587BC and the Jewish people were taken into exile as slaves in Babylon, the city lay ruined until their return, from around 538BC, when Jerusalem again became the capital for the Jewish tribes. But the city remained a target for stronger foreign powers, with Alexander the Great sacking the city in 332BC and the Romans invading and ruling in the decades immediately before the time of Jesus. At all of these stages, the Israelites were small in number and their kingdom ripe for foreign dominance: their capital was their greatest asset and attracted attention from thousands of miles away.

Herod the Great built the Second Temple around 30–20BC, and it lasted just 100 years until the Roman Emperor Titus completely razed the city and destroyed the temple in AD70, following a Jewish revolt against Roman rule. This period has been recorded at length by Josephus in his two major works, *The Jewish War* and *Antiquities of the Jews*. For a while, Jews were banned from even entering the city walls, but, by the time Emperor Constantine converted to Christianity in AD330, the city had again become the centre of Jewish life in Palestine.

Muslim Arabs first took the city by force in AD636—just a decade after the brand new religion of Islam had begun spreading out from its home in Mecca. This event ushered in almost 1400 years of Muslim rule, interrupted only by two centuries of Crusader conquest and reconquest between 1095 and 1291. The prophet Mohammed was believed to have ascended to heaven from the Temple Mount during his night journey in the early seventh century, thus establishing the holiness of the city for Muslims as well as for Jews and Christians. Muslim control lasted until 1917, when the British took Palestine from the Ottoman Turks, under a League of Nations mandate. The British withdrew in 1948, having promised self-determination for both Jews and Arabs; the establishment of the state of Israel followed a UN vote and a short but bitter armed struggle between the new Jewish Israelis and their Arab neighbours between 1945 and 1948. During the war of independence, the Israelis claimed and won much more territory than had been included in the original UN partition plan of 1947, turning many hundreds of thousands of Arabs into refugees who flocked to the surrounding states, especially to the Jordanian-controlled West Bank.

Even then, however, Jerusalem was not united, as half of the city (East Jerusalem, including the Old City) was still under Jordanian control. Only in 1967, after the Six-Day War, when Israel invaded and occupied the Palestinian territories of the Gaza Strip and West Bank, was the Old City returned to Jewish hands. A deliberate removal of many, but not all, Muslim Arabs took place in the Old City, and the modern Quarters as marked out today came into being, as did the new Arab areas of East Jerusalem. Jerusalem's New City, originally built along and off the Jaffa Road, began to grow as the Israelis planned a larger city, far removed from the constraints of the Old City.

Throughout its history, apart from the periods of exile, Jews lived and worshipped in their home city. For centuries, whoever ruled the city, Christians also came to pay homage. With so much change and rule by non-Jews, it's worth remembering that, apart from the Old City, today's Israeli capital is first and foremost a modern, 20th-century creation. The Old City dates mainly from no earlier than the 12th–14th centuries, which makes it difficult sometimes to identify the exact locations that relate to the time of Jesus. It's best just to accept that the Old City is not as it was in AD33 and understand that, while we may not be seeing the actual landmarks of Jesus' journey and life, we are at least in the right vicinity.

The Easter story

By the time Jesus got to know Jerusalem (at the height of Herod's Second Temple period), the city was known throughout the civilised world as a wealthy religious and trading capital. It had established itself as a place not only where different people came together but also where the Jewish people had their home. When Jesus arrived during Passover in late March, AD33, the Old City was crammed with pilgrims, all geared up for the annual festival that commemorates Moses' leadership of the Israelites out of Egypt. Then, as now, the Old City faced outward from its surrounding walls through four principal gates—today's Damascus Gate in the north, St Stephen's (or the Lions) Gate in the east, the Dung Gate in the south and the Jaffa Gate in the west. As well as the huge edifice of the Second Temple, the city's walls would probably have been much closer to the city than they are today, with the forces of the Roman occupation headquartered in the Antonia Fortress. For an excellent visualisation of the Old City at this time, check out the impressive scale model at the Israel Museum in Jerusalem.

The city was also the starting point for the new Christian sect after Jesus' death and resurrection.

Footsteps

If Simon Sebag Montefiore reckons that 'Jerusalem is the place where God meets man,' for Christians the city has a funny way of showing it. This is where Jesus was finally confronted, judged and executed by the Jewish and Roman authorities combined: each had a part to play in his death.

In his final week, Jesus and the disciples walked through today's West Bank to Jericho and Bethany before arriving on the Mount of Olives, overlooking Temple Mount. Next day, Jesus was fêted as he entered the city from the east, and, after visiting the temple, he based himself in the Kidron Valley. Here, he and his followers took part in the Passover celebrations along with their comrades and families. Yet within days the disciples' leader was dead—executed before his friends and family in the most brutal way—and the terrified disciples themselves were scattered. So much for God's 'holy city'.

Part of the paradox of Jesus' life was the fact that he was as Jewish as it was possible to be (directly descended from the House of David), yet he was not a native of Jerusalem and visited the city only a handful of times, to attend the major festivals. He was an outsider who had little time for the Jewish authorities based in the city and put little effort into engaging with them. As such, he was a threat to both the Jewish religious leaders and the occupying Roman forces. The Romans, while caring little about a young rabbi walking around the countryside, were alarmed by the prospect of this radical figure marching through the capital city and upsetting fragile relations with the locals. So Pilate, despite his personal reluctance to denounce Jesus, bowed to the demands of the Jewish elders when they and the Jerusalem crowds demanded Jesus' crucifixion.

So Pilate asked Jesus, 'Are you the king of the Jews?' 'You have said so,' Jesus replied. Then Pilate announced to the chief priests and the crowd, 'I find no basis for a charge against this man.' But they insisted, 'He stirs up the people all over Judea by his teaching. He started in Galilee and has come all the way here.' On hearing this, Pilate asked if the man was a Galilean. When he learned that Jesus was under Herod's jurisdiction, he sent him to Herod, who was also in Jerusalem at that time.
LUKE 23:3–7

Jerusalem undoubtedly has an identity problem, especially for Christians. Many locations mentioned in the Gospels, such as those around Galilee, are still identifiable on the ground today, but, as we have seen, this isn't true for locations in Jerusalem. The 'footprint' of the ancient city has altered time and again. However, when we walk the roads of the Old City, we are probably walking along routes that have always existed. Cities do not usually reinvent street patterns, no matter how old they are, especially when those street patterns reflect basic north–south and east–west axes.

It is impossible to excavate the Church of the Holy Sepulchre fully, although, when digs have taken place in the past, they have nearly always supported the site's claims—for example, by identifying the nature of the bedrock and discovering a first-century cemetery on the site. People often suspect, when they walk around the Old City, that there must be much more buried beneath their feet, and they are right—there is. One day we may have the technology to see through the earth and rock upon which Jerusalem is built and better identify evidence from 2000 years ago. However, until that day, we can continue to experience the special magic of the Old City for what it is, without doubting what speaks to our hearts.

The Easter story is played out mostly on the Mount of Olives to the east of the city walls, in the Kidron Valley below, in the Upper City of Jerusalem (the location of Herod's palace and the house of Caiaphas), where Jesus was brought after his arrest, and on the pathways in between. While it's entirely possible to identify the general vicinity of all these places today, trouble comes when we try to pin down exact locations, because not even the original source materials— the Gospels themselves—quite agree. Questions remain over the place of Pilate's residence and the exact site of Calvary, for example, as well as the home of Caiaphas.

It's likely, however, that Pilate was holed up in Herod's palace—on the site of today's Citadel by the Jaffa Gate. This would place Calvary a few hundred metres away, to the north of the Citadel, outside the city walls, either exactly at or close to the site of today's Church of the Holy Sepulchre—which carries much archaeological and geographical evidence for its claim to authenticity.

All of these assumptions at least make historical sense and have an amount of research to back them up. The site of the Holy Sepulchre is likely to be correct. In contrast, today's Via Dolorosa (running from the Antonia Fortress to the Holy Sepulchre) is unlikely to be the right route, because it starts on the wrong side of town and is simply too long. The route to the cross was much more likely to have gone across today's square in front of the Jaffa Gate, through the city's northern walls and out to a small mound on the edge of an old quarry or cemetery just beyond. It is pretty certain that Jesus would not and could not have walked west from the city walls to Calvary (a distance of one kilometre) while carrying a heavy cross.

Gethsemane and the Mount of Olives

Jesus went out as usual to the Mount of Olives, and his disciples followed him. On reaching the place, he said to them, 'Pray that you will not fall into temptation.' He withdrew about a stone's throw beyond them, knelt down and prayed, 'Father, if you are willing, take this cup from me; yet not my will, but yours be done.'
LUKE 22:39–42

Today's garden and Church of All Nations sit on the site of Gethsemane, reached by a short but steep walk downhill into the Kidron Valley from the Lions Gate. The church is new, barely a century old, but much more tantalising is the olive grove in the garden. The trees here were carbon dated in the 1980s, by the University of California, to just over 2000 years old. This olive grove may be the very place where Jesus and his disciples sat and waited out the nights of Holy Week. If only trees could talk!

This fact certainly has a profound effect on many visitors, and Gethsemane is, understandably, one of the most popular of the Jerusalem pilgrimage sites—so much so that it's very difficult to get the place to yourself. An early morning visit offers the best chance of finding some quiet time in the garden and the opportunity to soak up the dramatic atmosphere. This is not just the place where Jesus was betrayed and arrested but where he and the disciples spent much of Holy Week, beneath the city walls. While Jesus had previously stayed with his friends Mary, Martha and Lazarus in nearby Bethany, during Holy Week the garden became both accommodation and headquarters for Jesus and his disciples.

At daybreak the council of the elders of the people, both the chief priests and the teachers of the law, met together, and Jesus was led before them. 'If you are the Messiah,' they said, 'tell us.' Jesus answered, 'If I tell you, you will not believe me, and if I asked you, you would not answer. But from now on, the Son of Man will be seated at the right hand of the mighty God.' They all asked, 'Are you then the Son of God?' He replied, 'You say that I am.' Then they said, 'Why do we need any more testimony? We have heard it from his own lips.'

LUKE 22:66–71

Today's Church of All Nations was built with donations from countries around the world, hence the name. It can be a busy place but on a sunny day the light streaming in through the windows makes it a memorable one, too. Across the street is the Church of the Virgin Mary and also nearby is the Olive Press, site of an original first-century olive press, of the type in use at the time of Jesus.

Gethsemane itself is accessed through a small entrance in the high wall leading up the side street to the left (as you walk down the hill from the Old City), before the church. Further up the same road is a café and a couple of souvenir shops and a steep path up to the top of the Mount of Olives, which is definitely worth climbing for the view. For a less steep route, you take the first right immediately after the entrance to Gethsemane. On the way to the summit, you can pause and explore the sprawl of cemeteries and tombs spread out across the hillside. Halfway up, you will find the Church of Dominus Flevit, which commemorates the site where Jesus is said to have wept over the future of the city:

As he approached Jerusalem and saw the city, he wept over it and said, 'If you, even you, had only known on this day what would bring you peace—but now it is hidden from your eyes. The days will come upon you when your enemies will build an embankment against you and encircle you and hem you in on every side. They will dash you to the ground, you and the children within your walls. They will not leave one stone on another, because you did not recognize the time of God's coming to you.'
LUKE 19:41–44

From the top of the hill are famous views of the Old City and the Judean hills beyond. Directly behind the hill to the east is Bethany. You will always find a few fellow tourists and an old man in traditional Arab dress selling photo opportunities and rides upon his long-suffering donkey for a few shekels, but again it's nice to come early in the morning or late in the evening and enjoy the views without coachloads of day trippers getting in the way. For those who cannot undertake the steep walk up the hill, a taxi from the Old City to the Mount of Olives should cost no more than 15 or 20 NIS.

From up here it's easy to make out the topography of the city and imagine the events of Easter unfolding below. We know that Jesus and his disciples stopped up here themselves on many occasions, especially during the final week of Jesus' life, to take in the view and generally chill out. Like a vantage point over any city, the Mount of Olives allows you to understand some of the context of what is playing out below.

Each day Jesus was teaching at the temple, and each evening he went out to spend the night on the hill called the Mount of Olives.
LUKE 21:37

Mount Zion

Across the valley from the Mount of Olives and just outside the southern walls of the Old City is Mount Zion. Celebrated in the Bible as the highest point in the city and the original site for David's City, it is described in Psalm 48:1–2 as God's 'holy mountain, beautiful in its loftiness, the joy of the whole earth'.

Close to the city's Armenian Quarter, Mount Zion is also just a short walk (around ten minutes) to the south of the Jaffa Gate. On the way through, the Armenian Quarter reminds us that it is possible to get away from the hubbub of the Old City without having to leave its walls. As you walk past the Armenian Museum, it's worth a visit to understand the history of the Armenian people and their particular involvement in Jerusalem, past and present. The museum also includes details of the 1915 Armenian genocide, when up to 1.5 million Armenians were killed by the Ottoman Turks. You will find young Armenians still demonstrating in the streets and hanging political slogans from their buildings today.

The Mount Zion area contains a number of quieter tourist sites and is well worth a couple of hours of your time. Dominated by the Church of the Dormition, this is the place where the Virgin Mary is said to have died, or 'fallen asleep' (the root meaning of 'Dormition'). The church stands south of the Zion Gate, with the bell tower of the Hagia Maria Sion Abbey (formerly the Abbey of the Dormition), a Benedictine monastery, nearby and clearly visible as you approach. The path from the Zion Gate forks once (the Chamber of the Holocaust being on the left, downhill) and then forks again: the path leading to the Upper Room and David's Tomb is on the left, with the way to the church on the right.

The site of the Upper Room, like the other locations mentioned in the Easter story, is very difficult to authenticate, but this site claims to be on land once occupied by a traditional house that held a large upper room above the living quarters. Today the room pays homage to the Last Supper. It's a quiet place in a fine location overlooking the Kidron Valley and makes a great location to sit and read silently from the Bible.

On the Thursday evening of their week in the city, Jesus and the disciples ate a supper during which Jesus washed his disciples' feet and shared with them bread and wine, which he interpreted as symbols of the sacrifice he was soon to make.

When the hour came, Jesus and his apostles reclined at the table.
And he said to them, 'I have eagerly desired to eat this Passover
with you before I suffer. For I tell you, I will not eat it again until
it finds fulfilment in the kingdom of God.' After taking the cup,
he gave thanks and said, 'Take this and divide it among you. For
I tell you I will not drink again from the fruit of the vine until
the kingdom of God comes.' And he took bread, gave thanks and
broke it, and gave it to them, saying, 'This is my body given for
you; do this in remembrance of me.' In the same way, after the
supper he took the cup, saying, 'This cup is the new covenant in
my blood, which is poured out for you.'

LUKE 22:14–20

This Upper Room dates back to the eleventh century. When
Suleiman took the city 200 years later, he converted the
building into a mosque—hence the Arabic scroll on the
eastern wall. With the Tomb of David downstairs claiming to
be the last resting place of King David as well, this location
bears the marks of all three faiths. The Upper Room and
Tomb of David are both open from 8.00 am to 5.00 pm,
Sunday to Thursday, and entry is free. The nearby Harp of
David restaurant isn't cheap but is perfectly located if you
end up in this part of the city around lunch time and can't
walk back to Jaffa Gate or the New City before lunch.

The neighbouring Chamber of the Holocaust is a small but
historically significant museum. It was the first place in Israel
to commemorate the Holocaust and was set up by survivors
long before the Holocaust became a mainstream cultural
icon. It cannot possibly compare to the national Holocaust
Museum at Yad Vashem (see pages 70–72 for more details)
but it has a simple, moving dignity that cannot be ignored.
The dark, cave-like rooms are full of old black-and-white

laminated photographs and written narratives. Each plaque on the wall commemorates a community or family lost to the Holocaust. It's a world away from the modern museums in evidence elsewhere but is often quiet. The shaded courtyard and memorial rooms are open Sunday to Thursday, 8.00 am to 4.00 pm, and from 8.00 am to 1.00 pm on Fridays. A donation of 12 NIS per person is suggested. Wear a *kippa* (a skull cap, also known as a *yarmulke*) if you have one or can borrow one. Some eager touts are always selling them to tourists outside David's Tomb if you wish to buy yourself one.

Further down the hill, towards the Kidron Valley, you will see signs for the Church of St Peter in Gallicantu (open from 8.30 am to 5.30 pm every day except Sunday; no entry fee). This is the reported site of the house of Caiaphas, where Peter denied his association with Jesus three times before the cock crowed. The walk down to the church also includes some ancient stone steps, which date from the first century—almost certainly one of the routes that Jesus and the disciples would have taken from the Mount of Olives to Mount Zion any number of times during his last week. The church has an intriguing display of many chapels and rooms, including a cell and guardroom.

A servant girl saw [Peter] seated there in the firelight. She looked closely at him and said, 'This man was with him.' But he denied it. 'Woman, I don't know him,' he said. A little later someone else saw him and said, 'You also are one of them.' 'Man, I am not!' Peter replied. About an hour later another asserted, 'Certainly this fellow was with him, for he is a Galilean.' Peter replied, 'Man, I don't know what you're talking about!' Just as he was speaking, the cock crowed. The Lord turned and looked straight at Peter. Then Peter remembered the word the Lord had spoken to him: *'Before the cock crows today, you will disown me three times.' And he went outside and wept bitterly.*

LUKE 22:56–62

Lastly on Mount Zion, in the Catholic cemetery across the main road (follow the small road down from the Chamber of the Holocaust) is the grave of Oskar Schindler. Famous as a German and a member of the Nazi Party who saved over 1000 of his Jewish factory workers during World War II, he is buried here in Jerusalem and commemorated at Yad Vashem as being among the 'Righteous of the Nations'. The subject of the 1982 book *Schindler's Ark* by Thomas Keneally, which spawned the 1993 Steven Spielberg film *Schindler's List*, Oskar Schindler died almost penniless and unknown in 1974, yet his grave is now one of the most famous and often-visited in the city. From the entrance gate (behind the small car park), turn left and follow the rough path down to a set of semi-circular stone steps. At the bottom, look diagonally to your right and about 30 metres across the cemetery you will find Schindler's grave at the nearest end of a row.

Via Dolorosa

While it may be historically inaccurate, the current route of the Via Dolorosa proves very moving to groups re-enacting Jesus' journey along the cobblestones. It is in the remembering of this immensely painful part of Jesus' journey that we can reconnect with the Gospel accounts and put ourselves on the path with our Lord. Reading the relevant passages from the Gospels as you walk along the streets and alleyways of the Old City, following the 14 stations of the cross, can be a remarkable experience. Whether the journey is made alone or in a group, during the day or in the middle of the night, walking the Via Dolorosa is often a highlight for pilgrims.

As the soldiers led him away, they seized Simon from Cyrene, who was on his way in from the country, and put the cross on him and made him carry it behind Jesus. A large number of people followed him, including women who mourned and wailed for him. Jesus turned and said to them, 'Daughters of Jerusalem, do not weep for me; weep for yourselves and for your children.'
Luke 23:26–28

The Jerusalem stations of the cross (along the route of the Via Dolorosa) were first invented in medieval times in an attempt to encourage early Christian tourism and underline the Crusaders' claims to the city, and have fallen in and out of fashion over the centuries. They are placed mainly along a line devised by the Franciscans to satisfy European pilgrims wanting to take in each step of the passion story during the twelfth century. The stations roughly follow the chronology once Pilate has sent Jesus away to face his sentence, as set out in Matthew and Mark.

The soldiers led Jesus away into the palace (that is, the Praeto-rium) and called together the whole company of soldiers. They put a purple robe on him, then twisted together a crown of thorns and set it on him. And they began to call out to him, 'Hail, king of the Jews!' Again and again they struck him on the head with a staff and spat on him. Falling on their knees, they paid homage to him. And when they had mocked him, they took off the purple robe and put his own clothes on him. Then they led him out to crucify him.
Mark 15:16–20

The stations begin close to Lions Gate. The usual starting place is either the Ecce Homo convent or St Anne's Church, although the first station itself is along the street, inside the local school. Because the school is normally closed to visitors, you can often spot crowds milling outside the Crusader-era St Anne's Church instead. The Pool of Bethesda is next door.

Now there is in Jerusalem by the Sheep Gate a pool, which in Aramaic is called Bethesda, and which is surrounded by five covered colonnades. Here a great number of disabled people used to lie—the blind, the lame, the paralysed. One who was there had been an invalid for thirty-eight years. When Jesus saw him lying there and learned that he had been in this condition for a long time, he asked him, 'Do you want to get well?'

'Sir,' the invalid replied, 'I have no one to help me into the pool when the water is stirred. While I am trying to get in, someone else goes down ahead of me.'

Then Jesus said to him, 'Get up! Pick up your mat and walk.' At once the man was cured; he picked up his mat and walked.
JOHN 5:2–9

The second station is located at the Franciscan-run Chapel of the Flagellation. It is claimed that Jesus received the cross at this location. The next three stations are all close together on two corners of the main intersection at Al-Wad Road. This is a busy part of the Old City: to attach some serenity to the route, you may wish to walk it at different times of day, if you are spending several nights in town. A tiny chapel to the left of the gates on the corner of the junction holds the third station—where Jesus fell for the first time. Across the road is the fourth station, where Jesus is said to have seen his mother in the crowd. The point where an alleyway starts to run uphill off Al-Wad Road is the fifth station—where Simon was ordered to help carry the cross.

> *A certain man from Cyrene, Simon, the father of Alexander and Rufus, was passing by on his way in from the country, and they forced him to carry the cross.*
>
> MARK 15:21

The Via Dolorosa now climbs steadily all the way to Calvary. On the left, after around 25 deep steps, you will find the sixth station of the cross, where a woman traditionally named Veronica is said to have wiped Jesus' face with a cloth. Further along, after crossing the busy Souq Khan El-Zeit Street, you will find the seventh station, on the right-hand side of the alley, in a tiny chapel marked with signs on the stone wall alongside. This is where Jesus is said to have fallen for the second time under the crippling weight of his burden. Further along the same street, on the left, is the eighth station: a simple cross marks the spot where Jesus told the crowd not to cry for him but for themselves.

Now retrace your steps to the main street. Back at the intersection with Al-Wad Road, take a right turn and then make a dog-leg up a set of steps, also on the right, until you find yourself at the Coptic church. The ninth station is marked at the church's door. This is where Jesus is supposed to have fallen for the third time. Back on Khan El-Zeit Street, head south until you can turn right and come up past the bazaar and through the small arch to the Church of the Holy Sepulchre itself.

Inside is where you will find stations 10 to 14, all of them around the Chapel of Calvary, where Jesus was stripped of his clothes (the tenth) and nailed to the cross (the eleventh).

The site of the crucifixion is at station twelve (look for the cracked rock at the base of the altar) and the place where his body was laid out is at station 13. Back downstairs from the Chapel of Calvary is where you will find the 14th station—the tomb of Jesus—in the heart of the church's great rotunda. There is often a lengthy queue for this final station and, unfortunately, a bit of pushing and shoving: see pages 51–52 for more information on the issues surrounding the Church of the Holy Sepulchre and its competing guardians.

By the time you reach these final stations in the church itself, it may have felt like a gruelling journey for you too. On a hot day without enough food or water, one or two hours outside can leave you feeling wrecked—but just imagine how Jesus must have felt. Already flogged and humiliated, he struggled to carry his cross even the distance from Herod's palace to Golgotha.

They came to a place called Golgotha (which means 'the place of the skull'). There they offered Jesus wine to drink, mixed with gall; but after tasting it, he refused to drink it. When they had crucified him, they divided up his clothes by casting lots. And sitting down, they kept watch over him there. Above his head they placed the written charge against him: THIS IS JESUS, THE KING OF THE JEWS. Two rebels were crucified with him, one on his right and one on his left.

Matthew 27:33–38

A crowd had begun following Jesus and by now women were wailing at the brutality. Grown men were weeping for the humiliating end of their hopes and dreams. The political and religious zealots felt betrayed by Jesus, while the faithful felt betrayed by the Jewish high priests. As the cross was hauled up on the small mound at the edge of the city, dozens of people gathered, looking on, some hoping and praying for a miracle, some simply curious at who this man—placed firmly between two thieves, the lowest of the low—was, had been and would be.

Calvary itself can be a busy place, and, after a long trek along the Via Dolorosa, the ever-present crowds can mean it lacks serenity. If you find the crowds along the Via Dolorosa equally overwhelming, it is worth considering an alternative route. It may be more appealing to recreate the possible route to Golgotha from Herod's Palace (on the site of the present-day Citadel, by the Jaffa Gate). This can be done by following the Shivil Saint George and Hakoptin streets downhill to the Church of the Holy Sepulchre. It's certainly a shorter and less busy route, but no one has ever formalised it: therefore, if you are following it, you will need to improvise the location of the individual stations. Reading from Mark's Gospel will definitely help along the way, and you may find that walking your own route, rather than simply following scores of other Christians on the medieval Via Dolorosa, will result in a more personal journey.

Golgotha

The site of the Church of the Holy Sepulchre was outside the city walls in Jesus' time and on the summit of a small hill—no more than a mound—so it is perfectly feasible that this location could be the site of Calvary, or Golgotha. Golgotha was a first-century crucifixion site, coupled with a cemetery, next to an old quarry. Archaeological excavations have revealed all of those elements to be present here, as well as the small hill below what is now the Calvary Chapel.

Rock for building in Jerusalem was quarried from a number of small sites surrounding the city walls.

> *When they came to the place called the Skull, they crucified him there, along with the criminals—one on his right, the other on his left.*
>
> LUKE 23:33

The Garden Tomb (also known as Gordon's Calvary) is an alternative site, although there is little or no archaeological evidence to back up its claim. The setting, with a skull-like face in the side of the nearby cliff, and the tiny tomb inside the rockface, is certainly atmospheric, and it's a nice place to sit and read. It also has a useful bookshop. It's situated on Nablus Road, just behind the Damascus Gate but outside the city walls (open daily, 9.00 am to 5.30 pm, except on Sundays; free entry).

The Church of the Holy Sepulchre

The early church could keep their knowledge of the site of Calvary alive only by passing it on through word of mouth, since there were no other markers. Yet, as the church grew, Christians began to congregate there in greater numbers. Then, in AD135, the Romans built a temple dedicated to their goddess Venus, including a statue of Jupiter, on the site, hoping that this would prevent Christians from gathering and worshipping there. The first church was constructed on the same site in 325 by St Helena, mother of the Roman Emperor Constantine. The church was destroyed by the Persians in 614, rebuilt in 630 and destroyed again in 1009 by the Fatmid Caliph Al Hakim bi-Amr Allah, before being rebuilt yet again in 1048.

It is largely this building that survives today, with major renovations from 1555 and the 19th century much in evidence. Until recently, the church also contained many steel girders dating from the British mandate, which were put in place to support the rotunda after the earthquake of 1927. As a general rule, the deeper you go into the surviving building (down into the Helena Chapel, for example), the older it is. The very bottom of the basilica can be dated back to the 630 reconstruction, as it survived the destruction of 1009.

Despite being the most important site in all Christendom, a first visit to the church can sometimes be disappointing, to say the least. It is undoubtedly a frustrating place in the practical sense. Inside, it's a dark and confusing building, almost incomprehensible without a plan or guide to help you. The church can also be incredibly busy—at some times unbearably so, with pilgrims and even monks and clergy pushing and shoving people out of the way. There is, at times, a clear lack of respect and grace going on, which reflects the centuries of wrangling over ownership and use of the site—today split between the Armenian, Catholic, Greek Orthodox, Coptic and Ethiopian Churches, as well as the Franciscans. This rivalry over stewardship has created bad feeling among those tasked to look after the building and greet visitors, so the church has often been the scene of violent clashes between the different groups, none of which wishes to see a single centimetre of 'its' part of the church lost to a rival faction. As recently as 2008, a fight between Armenian and Greek Orthodox monks had to be broken up by dozens of armed police.

Interestingly, the keys to the church have been entrusted to two local Muslim families for the last 200 years, in order to prevent any of the factions from gaining full control of the site. Visit at 4.00 am and you may just catch the front door being unlocked.

The rivalry can be depressing, but it's worth persevering and paying a second and third visit if you are in the Old City over a number of days. The church can be a tranquil and peaceful place, especially first thing in the morning or late in the evening. Just after dawn, when the chants of the Franciscans can be heard, the space comes thrillingly alive. If you can climb the steps to Calvary (the site of the stone on which the cross is said to have been placed) when the church is quiet, and stand or sit before the shrine alone and think about the cross, it is unbearably moving. Similarly, the Stone of Anointing, just below the steps to the Calvary Chapel, receives more than its fair share of weeping pilgrims.

Key locations around the church include the final four stations of the cross, located around the Calvary Chapel (see pages 47–48). Down in the main rotunda is the site of Jesus' tomb: again, there is often a long queue, so try to visit first thing in the morning or last thing in the evening if you can. The Franciscans, in their chapel beyond the rotunda, are most likely to have a service in English, especially morning Mass. Look for notices outside the chapel itself for the week's programme.

The Western Wall

The spiritual heart of Judaism is a special place and can come as a big surprise to many, for its sheer unpretentiousness. An open-air synagogue, the wall is accessible to all, 24 hours a day, regardless of their background, with an amazingly tangible presence that seems to stay with you long after you've turned your back on it.

Regardless of your faith, it's very hard not to feel the pull and energy of this place, which gives off a vibe that can literally be felt. The way the great white stones of the wall store the heat of the day means that they are always warm to the touch, even at night. They give off a radiance that you can feel on your face, as if you were standing in front of a fire. It's this energy that affects the crowds of people who at times seem to overwhelm the site, and that will probably make you return time and again. The wall is, in a word, addictive.

Footsteps

The very first time I visited the Holy Land, I arrived at Ben Gurion airport around 4.00 am, and as soon as I left the terminal I took a *sherut* straight to Jerusalem. Too early to check into my hostel and too excited to enjoy a leisurely breakfast in one of the early morning cafés on Jaffa Street, I hitched my rucksack on to my back and headed for the Old City on foot.

By the time I was walking the cobblestones it was 5.30 am and the church bells and muezzins had begun their first calls of the day. It was still dark as the religious early risers began to pass me in the street, and, as they headed downhill, I decided to follow. A group of black-clad men quickly led me through a zigzag of alleyways, the marble paths polished by centuries of shoe leather, until I came to a tiny checkpoint perched above an open square. As the sun was just beginning to turn the eastern sky pink beyond the city's walls, I showed my passport, had my bag X-rayed and followed the steps down to the Western Wall itself. I donned a skullcap and stood right in front of the great white stones, feeling their heat on my face. By the time the sun was up, the plaza was full of worshippers, many

Orthodox, but most not. Some were businessmen in suits on their way to work, others in their army fatigues, still others in jeans and T-shirts.

Thankful to have arrived safely and to have come across this experience as my very first interaction with Jerusalem, I took a few steps back and sat on one of the plastic chairs scattered across the plaza, bowed my head and began to pray.

The Western Wall is the only remains of the Second Temple and still makes up one of the retaining walls of the Temple Mount. The Dome of the Rock now adorns the plateau above, but the stones at the foot of the wall date from Solomon's (First Temple) time, with the higher (larger) stones from Herod's Second Temple. It's easy to see the difference when you look up.

On the left of the plaza in front of the wall is a bookshop, toilets and a tunnel that runs north towards Aqbat e Saraya Street; on the right is the entrance to the Western Wall Tunnels. A visit needs to be booked online, well in advance (the cost is 30 NIS), but the tunnels are worth the effort. They reveal the archaeological foundations at the base of the Temple Mount and help to tell the fascinating story of the city and its greatest religious monument.

The tunnels are the result of ongoing archaeological work, which has turned up a lot of information about the way this part of the city (essentially a steep valley) was filled in to create the more level ground we see today. Standing before a stone the size of a double-decker bus, weighing 500 tonnes, several metres underground, really brings the archaeology of the city to life.

Temple Mount and the Dome of the Rock

Above the Western Wall sits one of the most sacred sites in Islam—the Dome of the Rock. It's from here that the prophet Mohammed is said to have crowned his 30-year ministry on earth by ascending to heaven. That the event happened here, in the home of the two other monotheistic faiths, reminds us of the very close relationship shared by each religion with the others, as well as the fact that for more than half of its history Jerusalem has been ruled by Muslims, who were still in charge until 1967. The conflict between the three faiths is part of the reality of the Holy Land, and the Temple Mount has, in recent times, been closed for long periods. Like the city at whose heart it stands, it symbolises the constant tug-of-war for this corner of the world.

The way Judaism, Islam and Christianity rub shoulders in Jersualem throws up some fascinating scenarios. The Israeli government controls access to the Dome of the Rock, while two Muslim families (as we've already seen) hold the keys to the Church of the Holy Sepulchre. Christians make up the vast majority of pilgrim visitors to the Holy Land, yet those pilgrims almost completely ignore the indigenous Christian communities here, which continue to shrink and, perhaps rightly, sometimes feel forgotten by their Western fellow believers.

The Temple Mount plaza offers one of the only open spaces in the whole city. Non-Muslims can access the site only from the Western Wall plaza (look for the wooden walkway), although you may exit by the more northerly entrances, by the Via Dolorosa and beneath the site of the Roman Antonia Fortress. This fortress was a kind of occupier's barracks or police station, of vital importance in Jesus' time as the Romans attempted to keep an eye on activity within the temple compound. The open plaza of the Temple Mount makes a huge contrast to the warren of streets and alleys below, and, on a hot day, the sun can be blinding. We know that Jesus walked on this plaza, famously in anger at one point—an episode recounted in all four Gospels. Pilgrims today may well understand how he felt after the fourth or fifth hawker of the day has tried to sell them a scarf or robe there. Although the location then took a very different form, the giant rocks used to build the mount all date from Herod's time or earlier, so your feet may be walking in the very footsteps of Jesus.

> *When Jesus entered the temple courts, he began to drive out those who were selling. 'It is written,' he said to them, '"My house will be a house of prayer"; but you have made it "a den of robbers".' Every day he was teaching at the temple. But the chief priests, the teachers of the law and the leaders among the people were trying to kill him. Yet they could not find any way to do it, because all the people hung on his words.*
>
> LUKE 19:45–48

The Al-Aqsa mosque at the southern end of the plaza may be open for visits, although you should dress fully covered and be prepared to leave your shoes, bags and camera at the door. To the north, across the great plaza, stands the oldest and perhaps most recognisable Islamic building in the world. Having survived attacks, earthquakes and wear and tear since AD650, the Dome of the Rock is one of the most fascinating buildings on earth. Normally closed to visitors, it may be possible to seek entry if you're humble and polite with the guardian: again, being fully covered will increase your chances of being let in. The rotunda is a dark but tranquil place inside, with the bare bedrock at the centre of the mosque visible from the basement. This is the spot where Abraham got ready to sacrifice Isaace and also the site of Mohammed's ascension to heaven during his night journey. According to Old Testament tradition, this very rock is the foundation stone of the whole earth. It was also the site of the altar in both temples and there has been worship carried out here, in one form or another, pretty much continuously for over 3000 years.

On Fridays, when the Al-Aqsa mosque is in full use, there can be many thousands of people on the plaza, although non-Muslim visitors cannot visit then. During the rest of the week, the plaza is often a quiet and tranquil place, in contrast to the rest of the Old City. Most visitors will be Western tourists and pilgrims. There would probably be many more Muslim pilgrims coming here but for the fact that the Israeli government controls access to the area, and at times in the past, especially during violent confrontations between Israelis and Palestinians elsewhere in the country, opportunities to visit the site have been restricted.

The Muslim Quarter

North of the plaza and pulsing with life, the Muslim Quarter is the Old City at its rambunctious best. With some great restaurants serving aromatic meats as well as the best hummus and Mediterranean salads you've ever tasted, eating is top of the list of things to do here. Many Muslim Arab families still live here too, as a walk north on any of the alleyways off the Via Dolorosa will reveal.

The Damascus Gate is the second-busiest route into the Old City after the Jaffa Gate and has a pleasant amphitheatre plaza immediately in front of it. The alleyway through the gate reveals the classic Crusader defensive zigzag design. Back through the souq is one of the Old City's most famous eating establishments: at the bottom of the steps where the route from the gate splits in two is Hamid's falafel shop. From this simple, tiny stall, the owner works all day producing the city's best falafels, which also happen to be the cheapest, at just 8 NIS. The average price for a falafel in the rest of the city is between 12 and 15 NIS.

As well as the restaurants listed on pages 65–66, try out one of the many fresh juice stalls dotted along Al-Had Street or grab a welcome ice cream as you take a break from walking the Via Dolorosa.

City walls

A walk along the top of the city's walls is a great way not just to see Jerusalem but also to get away from the city's crowds. A full circuit will take a couple of hours, so beware the heat and ensure you have a bottle of water, a hat and sunscreen with you. Again, early morning visits tend to be the most rewarding, with few other tourists present.

The walls are accessible from several points and one of the nice things about them is the possibility of picking up a section of the wall after you've been visiting another part of the city. A walk on the walls can be combined with a visit to the Temple Mount, for example, or Mount Zion. Access to the southern section from behind the Citadel costs 16 NIS and closes at 5.00 pm. Local kids may be hanging round the northern section, keen to show you shortcuts: they'll expect a couple of shekels if you take them up on their offer, but don't be afraid to ignore them if they are bothering you.

The original walls date from Solomon's time, with a second set of city walls constructed around 400BC and a third set from Herod's time, subsequently rebuilt during the reign of Suleiman in AD1400. The current walls date from 1400 and follow a line that is an amalgam of all of the previous versions. The walls once reached much further north and south, encompassing parts of the city such as Mount Zion, which are now outside the city walls.

Jaffa Gate and the Citadel

Perhaps the busiest route into and out of the Old City, the Jaffa Gate is now part of the Citadel, itself built on the remains of Herod's Palace. Excavations at the site have revealed even older walls dating back to Solomon's time.

The Citadel (or Tower of David Museum, to give it its official title) now tells the story of the city through the ages and is well worth exploring for a couple of hours. Admission is a hefty NIS 46, but worth it for the views of the Old City alone (opening times are 9.00 am to 5.30 pm every day except Saturday). Another good reason to visit the museum is found in the basement in the form of a 19th-century scale model of the city by Hungarian artist Stephen Illes. There's also a shady café, which provides an affordable lunch or snack stop.

There are plenty of shops and restaurants around the Jaffa Gate, as well as a post office and the well-resourced Christian Information Centre, run by the Franciscans, both opposite the main entrance to the Tower of David Museum. Inside the Jaffa Gate itself is also an official Tourist Information Centre, open Sunday–Friday. There are a couple of ATMs in the area, plus the traditional money changers and usual street hawkers. There are further ATMs and restaurants inside the new Mamilla Mall, just two minutes' walk outside the Jaffa Gate, where you can find fashionable stores and good-value restaurants that target locals as well as tourists.

Haggling is a cultural necessity in Israeli markets and Arab shops, as it is throughout the Middle East. A general guide is to aim to pay around 30–40 per cent of the original quoted price, although it may take you a long time to get to that point. Be aware that as soon as you begin asking the price of a particular item, you're communicating to the shop owner your intention to buy it, and changing your mind will represent loss of face for the person selling. Shopkeepers may well ply you with drinks and sweets and want to chat before the deal is done: shops are a social meeting point as well as a commercial one. If you're not prepared for this, it's best just to stay away from craft and souvenir shops altogether and be polite but firm when refusing the hawkers on the street. To get into an argument or lose your temper in such a situation would be to break a major cultural taboo. No matter how mock-offended a shopkeeper may appear, haggling should always be done with good humour at its core. At the same time, always keep a close eye on your change, because there is a local habit of rounding up any kind of bill by a few shekels. Similarly, if using your credit card, look out for any last-minute surcharges or even changes in currency (such as from shekels to pounds or dollars), which should ring alarm bells.

Heading north of Jaffa Gate brings you straight into the Christian Quarter and, by zigzagging continually uphill past many Orthodox pilgrim hostels, you will eventually come out at New Gate. Walking south from Jaffa Gate gets you quickly into the quieter streets of the Armenian Quarter, with its Armenian museum and access through the city walls to Mount Zion beyond (see page 41). Every other direction (essentially, any street that runs downhill) is headed for the heart of the Old City.

Inbound and outbound travel details

All Egged and other long-distance buses terminate at Jerusalem's central bus station in the New City. Arab buses terminate at the bus station opposite the Damascus Gate. From the central bus station it's a 45-minute walk or ten-minute tram ride to Damascus Gate and the edge of the Old City; you can also catch the No.1 bus. To reach Jaffa Gate, most people walk down Jaffa Street and through the Mamilla shopping mall. If you've caught the tram to Damascus Gate, simply follow the wall round. A taxi can also drop you at the steps at the bottom of the mall but be aware that, at rush hour, it's much quicker to get through Jerusalem on foot.

Walking is the only option for accessing the vast majority of sites in the Old City, so good footwear is essential. It is definitely not a place for flipflops or sandals. With countless steps and narrow, crowded alleyways, it is difficult for those with limited mobility, although the Western Wall has good disabled access. The only saving grace is that distances are small: the Old City stretches barely a kilometre across. Watch the stone steps of streets like David Street if it rains: they can be treacherously slippy.

The train station is currently at Malkha, next to the Jerusalem Maccabees football stadium and Jerusalem Mall.

Accommodation in the Old City

Accommodation within the Old City is fairly limited and, though over-priced, is worth the expense if you want to wake up with the sights and sounds of the great religious monuments right outside your window. Better-value deals can be found just outside the Old City walls, although you can expect to pay through the nose for top-end hotels.

Budget

There is not a great choice of accommodation within the walls of the Old City itself, so the budget accommodation on offer becomes a more appealing option than elsewhere. The hostels centred around Jaffa Gate and running downhill towards the centre of the Old City all provide affordable rooms and shared dormitories.

Citadel Hostel (the first choice for many), New Petra Hostel and the Jaffa Gate Hostel are all of similar quality, charging around £15 a night for a shared dormitory and £40 for a private room. They all feature viewing terraces, which allow you to catch some great photo opportunities across the rooftops or the chance to have some quiet time to yourself, especially at sunrise and sunset.

Standard

For the next step up, try the Imperial Hotel or Gloria Hotel, both directly opposite the Citadel's main tower. These both charge around £60 per night for a double en-suite room with breakfast and, although the interior decor is somewhat tired, they benefit from a pretty much perfect location.

The Rivoli Hotel, National Hotel and Metropole Hotel, north of Damascus Gate, all charge around £50 per night for a double room. In the same neighbourhood are a number of big mid-range hotels, some better than others: check out the Grand Court Jerusalem (part of a modern 'campus' of three large hotels close to the US Embassy and St George's Cathedral) and the Addar Hotel (on the same street), which are a ten-minute walk from Damascus Gate.

Back within the city walls, there are a number of Christian guesthouses in the Christian Quarter, which charge around £100 per night for a double room, usually with breakfast. Some are easier to find and book than others: many of the Orthodox pilgrimage houses accept bookings only from an Orthodox travel organisation.

One of the best (and best located) of the more accessible pilgrimage houses is the Lutheran Guest House (opposite the Citadel Hostel on the same alleyway, St Mark's, parallel to David Street), which has single rooms from £60 per night. Book via email: info@guesthouse-jerusalem.co.il.

Another good-quality location is the Casa Nova Franciscan's House for Pilgrims, uphill from Jaffa Gate and just further along from Greek Patriarch Street (go up the narrow alley at the junction with Casa Nova Street). It can be contacted by phone on +972-2-6282791, or email casanovaj@custodia. org. If it has space, you'll find yourself mixing with plenty of fellow Christian pilgrims and perhaps sharing in some impromptu Bible readings. Single rooms are £50 and doubles £70 per night.

The Christ Church Guesthouse, next to the Christian Information Centre by Jaffa Gate, is also worth a try. It has double rooms from around £110 per night (no unmarried couples allowed) and is run by evangelical mission group CMJ (www.cmj-israel.org).

If you want to be close to the Via Dolorosa, try the Ecce

Homo Convent hospice, which has over 100 guest rooms from £50 per night. This is one of the few places (Notre Dame is another) which may be able to accommodate walk-in customers, but don't count on it. It's best to contact them in advance, through www.eccehomoconvent.org.

Another Christian hospice along the Via Dolorosa is the Austrian Hospice, which again has rooms from around £50 per night and also has an excellent café/restaurant open to guests and non-guests (www.austrianhospice.com).

The enormous 400-room Pontifical Institute Notre Dame of Jerusalem Center (Notre Dame for short) is run by the Vatican and is just outside the city walls, between the Jaffa and Damascus Gates. It charges £70 per night for a single and £105 for a double room with buffet breakfast. There are two tram stops (City Hall and Damascus Gate) nearby.

Luxury

Of Jerusalem's top-end hotels, the King David and the Mamilla are among the closest to the Old City, a five-minute walk from Jaffa Gate, with double rooms from £250 per night, including high-quality breakfast. Jerusalem has a huge selection of top-end hotels, many of them in a part of the New City that allows easy access to the Old, so, if budget is not an issue, you will undoubtedly find an excellent, well-located place to stay.

Eating, drinking and shopping

As already mentioned, haggling is part of the culture, so, if you wish to go shopping in the souqs of the Old City, be forewarned. You will find an endless supply of the same T-shirts, figurines and gifts in almost every shop: choice is not a big part of the offer here. Of more genuine appeal may be jewellery or Arab scarves. Try to ignore the spa shops selling potions from the Dead Sea: you can find these products for sale across Israel in supermarkets at a fraction of the price.

Eating out is a little easier to organise: simply try to avoid anywhere which is occupied only by tourists. Two excellent indoor covered restaurants are Al-Nasser's (closer to Damascus Gate) or Al-A'Elat (Family) restaurant (closer to David Street), both on Beit Ha'bad Street. They are great value and less touristy than some other places, and won't rip you off. Jacob's Pizza and the other options on Latin Patriarch's Street (first left after Jaffa Gate) are also decent.

A walk down to the Mamilla Mall will bring you to a string of terraced restaurants with Western menus and prices to match. One area that is geared more towards inflated prices than good service is the covered bazaar known as the Muristan, immediately before the street that leads to the courtyard in front of the Church of the Holy Sepulchre. These cafés and shops make a living from daytrippers and are best avoided, which is a shame because the marbled streets and covered market stalls certainly look appealing and carry a fascinating history. Many of the buildings are converted Crusader-era Hospitaller hospices. Just be careful on these streets: not all that glitters is gold.

For a chilled-out vibe with a *sheesha* pipe later in the evening, try the Panorama Restaurant on the roof of one of the Muristan buildings. The Jerusalem Star Restaurant on Al-Wad Street is a lively place for a drink or game of pool with the locals—but be prepared to be thrashed every time!

The Old City is not a great place for nightlife, but the New City will amply reward you if serious restaurants, nightclubs and bars are more your thing. King George Street at the intersection with Ben Yehuda tends to be the hub of the action, but there is also a cluster of good bars around Ben Shetakh and Havilio Square, just off Jaffa Road, 15 minutes' walk from Jaffa Gate.

Falafels are the standard daytime snack in Israel but, if you're a meat eater, the ubiquitous kebab can be found in all sorts of varieties—schwarma, sheesh and kofta. These snacks are also served in restaurants as full plates for a meal and come with fresh salads featuring lots of hummus, parsley and tomatoes. Anyone who's a fan of chef Yotam Ottolenghi will delight in the robust flavours of Arab and Israeli cuisine and its inexpensive credentials. A full evening meal in one of the restaurants above or at others in the Arab Quarter should cost no more than 50 NIS per head. Just remember that you may not be able to drink alcohol with your meal.

In the bigger shops, prices should be on display, but ask before you get to a till if no prices are marked, even in the small supermarkets that line the alleyways. Food can be cheap but ice creams and drinks will be comparable to or dearer than they are back home. Feel free to try to haggle even over basic items such as water or biscuits. You won't offend anyone by trying.

Further reading

Simon Sebag Montefiore, *Jerusalem: The Biography* (Phoenix, 2012).

William Dalrymple, *From the Holy Mountain* (Flamingo, 1998).

Nick Page, *The Longest Week* (Hodder & Stoughton, 2009).

William Whitson (trans.), *New Complete Works of Josephus* (Kregel Academic, 1999).

Colin Chapman, *Whose Holy City?* (Lion Hudson, 2004).

–Chapter 3–

Jerusalem New City

With its excellent museums and distinctive Israeli culture, the New City has lots to offer the traveller. The new tramline has brought the main attractions and the Old City in closer proximity to one another.

- ✤ Introduction
- ✤ Israel Museum
- ✤ Knesset
- ✤ Yad Vashem
- ✤ Abu Ghosh and Ein Kerem
- ✤ Eating, drinking and shopping
- ✤ Travel details
- ✤ Accommodation in the New City

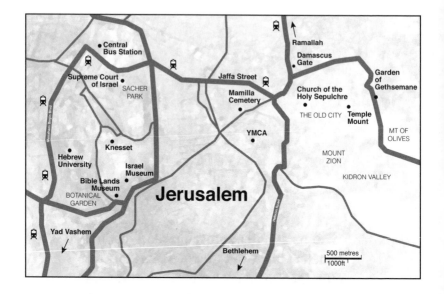

Map of Jerusalem showing: Central Bus Station, Supreme Court of Israel, SACHER PARK, Ramallah, Damascus Gate, Jaffa Street, Mamilla Cemetery, Garden of Gethsemane, Church of the Holy Sepulchre, THE OLD CITY, Temple Mount, MT OF OLIVES, YMCA, Knesset, Hebrew University, Israel Museum, MOUNT ZION, KIDRON VALLEY, Bible Lands Museum, BOTANICAL GARDEN, **Jerusalem**, Yad Vashem, Bethlehem, 500 metres / 1000ft

Introduction

For locals, Jerusalem is all about the New City. It contains everything they could ever need, and the same is true for visitors. There are enough sites here to warrant a visit even without the pull of the Old City. The museums are world class, the markets and nightlife upbeat, and getting around is easy.

The city centre is strung out along Jaffa Street and the streets that run off it. This area includes most of the accommodation options and the city's most obvious eateries and shops, which occupy the middle part of the street. The tram runs along Jaffa Street (see detailed travel section on pages 74–75), helping to connect the Old City, via Damascus Gate, with the city centre and central bus station, which sits towards the end of the city centre. From the stop opposite the convention centre, the museums and Knesset (parliament) are within 20 minutes' walking distance.

Sometimes the two parts of the city can seem worlds apart from one another. The Old City is all-absorbing and feels so vibrant when you are actually in it, yet the real life of Jerusalem is often taking place somewhere else. The Old City is dead after dark, whereas the streets around Ben Yehuda and Solomon Street and around Mahane Yehuda market are only just then coming alive.

Israel Museum

This fine museum is famous for several key exhibits, including the remains of many of the Dead Sea Scrolls found at Qumran in 1979 and a huge model of the Old City during the Second Temple era (when Jesus was alive here). The model is complete with houses, palaces, the Temple Mount and extended city walls, showing Jerusalem at its ancient height, just before the Jewish revolt in AD70 prompted the Romans to raze the city.

The model alone is worth the admission, but the museum also helps to tell the story of Israel from year dot to the present day. There are archaeological displays underlining the country's importance to the evolution and development of humankind. The region played a central role in establishing agriculture and the first steps towards urbanisation throughout the vital 'fertile crescent', which incorporated the lands of ancient Egypt, the Levant (Israel, Lebanon and Syria) and stretched across to Babylon (Iraq), and the museum tracks this evolutionary journey in great detail.

There are also contemporary art galleries and an outdoor sculpture trail to keep you occupied for more than a few hours. It's also a good place to walk around and take in the fine views of the rest of the city, especially to the south. Along with Yad Vashem, the museum is fully accessible for those with limited mobility. Across the road is the Bible Lands Museum (admission 40 NIS, open 9.00 am to 5.00 pm every day), which helps to give an accurate account of Israel's history during biblical times and, again, tells the story of the patriarchs, the kings and the time of Jesus.

To reach the Israel Museum, catch bus No.17 on King George Street, near Jaffa Street and Jaffa Central tram stop. It is open daily from 9.30 am to 5.30 pm, except on Fridays, when it closes at 2.00 pm. The entry fee is 48 NIS.

Knesset

A ten-minute walk from the museums above is the Israeli parliament, the Knesset. Its impressive interior is open for tours only on Sundays and Thursdays, from 9.30 am to 2.30 pm. Bring your passport for ID and get ready to photograph the Chagall-designed interior and the huge bronze *menorah* (seven-pronged candelabra) outside at the front of the Knesset—a gift from the British parliament in 1956.

Yad Vashem

The museum buildings themselves here are dramatic enough: the main galleries are shaped like a triangular prism (representing half a Star of David, to show how Europe's Jewish population was halved by the Nazis and their conspirators) thrusting through the side of a hill, with stunning views of the valleys spreading west of the city on its far side.

If the building design doesn't make the penny drop, once

inside, the subject matter will convince you that this is one of the most important museums in the world as well as one of the most stunning. The narrative tells the story first of the history of the Jewish populations of Europe and then their persecution, deportation and mass murder during World War II.

It's a forthright account, as you would expect, and pulls no punches in terms of its detail or its criticism of those who failed to act, including the Church and the West. Although there were many examples of Christians helping Jews during World War II, there were, unfortunately, more examples of Christians taking part in the Holocaust. The narrative at Yad Vashem also freely criticises the Allies for their lack of intervention during the Nazi crisis, especially towards the end of the war when information about what was happening was finally getting through to London and Washington.

The events of the Holocaust show very few people in a good light, and this reminds us that the need for a new home for so many Jews displaced in the war contributed directly to the creation of the state of Israel. This is often seen as a tenuous link and one that some historians reject, but Yad Vashem does suggest reasons why the Jewish state came into being when it did, with the backing of a bruised and battered international community. Many people forget, however, that the Holocaust was a taboo subject for decades, even among Israelis. Only after the Eichmann trial, which took place in Jerusalem in 1968, did the Holocaust begin to have common cultural and historical currency. This development continued during the 1980s and 1990s, with mainstream TV and then Hollywood making it a common cultural theme by the turn of the millennium. The growing awareness of the Holocaust is evident inside Israel itself, where local schoolchildren and

IDF members seem to make up the majority of visitors to Yad Vashem on weekdays.

To find Yad Vashem, catch the tram to the final southern stop (Mount Herzl) and walk down the road through the woods for ten minutes to the main entrance. The museum is open from 9.00 am to 6.00 pm every day except Saturday, with free entry. Allow at least half a day to walk through, or longer if you are interested in visiting the excellent research centre and bookshop behind the turning circle at the entrance.

Abu Ghosh and Ein Kerem

These suburbs of Jerusalem are often overlooked in favour of further-flung daytrips, but a combined day out west to these villages can be a highlight of a trip to Israel. Biblically important, Abu Ghosh is the place where the ark of the covenant was said to have lain for 20 years. The modern church of Our Lady of the Ark of the Covenant stands on the site of a much older Byzantine church whose mosaics can still be seen inside. Overlooking the town are also the impressive Crusader remains of a citadel, church and monastery built in 1142, marking the location of a fabled Roman legion who helped to capture and then defend the city during the Second Crusade.

Abu Ghosh is also a possible location for Emmaus, where the resurrected Lord appeared to two of his disciples, three days after his death.

Now that same day two of them were going to a village called Emmaus, about seven miles from Jerusalem. They were talking with each other about everything that had happened. As they

talked and discussed these things with each other, Jesus himself
came up and walked along with them; but they were kept from
recognising him.
LUKE 24:13–16

At Ein Kerem, churches dedicated to John the Baptist
and his mother Elizabeth are a draw for pilgrims who are
interested in seeing more of the locations connected with this
remarkable and sometimes overlooked figure in Jesus' life.
John was reportedly born here and raised on the outskirts
of Jerusalem, where he took a growing interest in the life of
the Second Temple and took regular pilgrimage trips on foot
into the city, where he spoke freely with rabbis and traders.
Although he spent much of his adult life in the Jordan Valley,
it was here in this much quieter and greener valley that he
spent his formative years. In that respect, his childhood and
his development into a public figure reflect the experiences
of Jesus himself.

Today the villages are Arab Muslim centres famed for their
food, including some of the best hummus in the Middle
East—so claimed by Ibrahim's restaurant on the main street
in Abu Ghosh. Many Jerusalemites of every community
travel out here just to sample the deliciously rich hummus,
which is constantly being made in full view at the restaurants.
Tourists are beginning to get in on the act too, although on
most days you will be pleasantly outnumbered by locals as
they crowd around their favourite eating place and spend
an entire afternoon eating, drinking and generally relaxing.

To get there, take a taxi, catch the No. 55 Egged bus from
the central bus station in Jerusalem or join an organised trip
such as those offered at the Abraham Hostel.

Eating, drinking and shopping

Some hotspots around Ben Yehuda include a number of good falafel shops on King George Street, with Sam's Bagels famously also on the corner of the same street. Nearby is a taxi office and the Nesher *sherut* office, at 23 Ben Yehuda, should you need to prebook your transport in person (useful on *Shabbat*).

Mahane Yehuda market is the epicentre of Jerusalem's culinary world, with fresh produce not just on display but also available to eat in the nearby restaurants and cafés. The standard Middle Eastern foods, such as hummus, *kibbe, baba-ghanoush*, and *tabouleh*, may be served up as a mezze (starter) or as a main course. There are several good restaurants around the market, such as Hashipudia, serving up several different kinds of kebab. If you're bored of local food, go to the excellent Ichikidana Indian restaurant, which specialises in *thali* (set meals).

The city's main shopping streets are Jaffa Street and Ben Yehuda and the streets round about. Jerusalem Mall in the south of the city is the main out-of-town shopping centre (take a No. 6 bus).

Travel details

From the central bus station (which will also be the terminus for the new deep-tunnel high-speed rail line from Tel Aviv and Ben Gurion, currently under construction), the New City is an easily walkable distance.

The very centre of the New City is Zion Square, where Jaffa Street intersects with Ben Yehuda Street, both of which are packed with pavement cafés. If you have time, one good way of orientating yourself with the city is to jump on the tram and travel from one end of the line to the other. The journey takes about 45 minutes and costs 6.60 NIS for a ticket. This is the same price as for the bus, although bus tickets are valid for 90 minutes so can be used to transfer within that time. The tram also underlines political issues: the line's northern end passes through occupied West Bank territory and travels through the largest Israeli settlement in East Jerusalem, Pisgat Ze'ev, which is deemed illegal under international law.

Currently, all trains into Jerusalem terminate at Malkha Station, next to Teddy Stadium and the Jerusalem Mall. This is some way out of town: a 25–30 NIS taxi fare will get you up to Jaffa Gate or further west on to Jaffa Road. Definitely don't try to walk it with heavy bags! The No. 6 bus will take you there and back from the central bus station.

The most straightforward route between the Old City and the New is out through Jaffa Gate, through the Mamilla Mall and then along Jaffa Road—in total, around 20–30 minutes' walking time. Add another 10–15 minutes if you wish to walk all the way to the central bus station, which is at least a mile and a half (2 km) from Jaffa Gate. A taxi should cost no more than 20 NIS for this journey, or you can hop on the bus or the tram.

Accommodation in the New City

There is no shortage of accommodation in the New City, whatever your budget, and hotels here are generally better value than those in or around the Old City. The area also has proper budget options, which don't exist elsewhere in the city.

Budget

The Jerusalem Guest House Hotel and Hostel has an unbeatable location in the middle of Jaffa Road, which gives this place the edge. It's smart and clean, although a little pricey for those on a really tight budget. Dormitory beds cost from £20, with private singles from £50.

The official HI Israeli youth hostel is located down in the German Colony, to the south-west of the Old City. It's a big, bright building close to Bloomfield Gardens (with excellent views over the Old City) and costs £20 per night for a dorm, £60 per night for a private room.

When it comes to hostels and budget hotels, there is no better place than the Abraham Hostel. It's definitely the most keenly priced, next to the tram stop on Davidka Square. The rooms are spotless and there are lots of communal areas, with everything you could ever wish for—a bar, laundry, bike hire, kitchen, travel agency, internet gallery, rooftop terrace, TV lounge and more. Dorms are priced from just £15, private rooms with en-suite from £40.

Standard

The Grand Court, Leonardis and Tamar are all similarly priced, mid-range establishments to the north of Damascus Gate, starting at £60 per night, including breakfast.

The Seven Arches and Mount of Olives hotels are also similarly priced and are both well located if you're after a stunning sunrise or sunset view of the Old City from the summit of the Mount of Olives. Double rooms start from £50 per night, including breakfast at both. The neighbourhood is a bit scruffy, however, and not very busy at night, making it perhaps less suitable for single travellers. Both hotels have seen better days. The Arches has bigger rooms, but the staff at the Mount of Olives are friendlier in my experience.

Luxury

The King David and Mamilla hotels have already been mentioned for their excellent service and their location close to the Old City. Both have pools, gyms and business facilities, and their superb restaurants are worth a visit even if you can't afford to stay the night. Expect to pay around £250 per night for a room at one of these 5-star establishments.

The American Colony hotel is another top player but in a very different location—close to St George's Cathedral in East Jerusalem and not far from the Damascus Gate. It has a lovely pool and cool, whitewashed rooms, from £150 per night including breakfast.

Further reading

Colin Chapman, *Whose Promised Land?* (Lion Hudson, 2002).
Simon Sebag Montefiore, *Jerusalem: The Biography* (Phoenix, 2012).
Yotam Ottolenghi and Sami Tamimi, *Jerusalem* (Ebury Press, 2012).

–Chapter 4–

Bethlehem and the West Bank

A guide to Bethlehem and the West Bank, Jesus' birthplace and the area where the reality of Arab-Israeli history comes vividly to life.

- ❖ Introduction
- ❖ Bethlehem
- ❖ The Church of the Nativity
- ❖ Shepherds' Fields
- ❖ Herodian
- ❖ Hebron
- ❖ Ramallah
- ❖ Taybeh
- ❖ Nablus
- ❖ Mount Gerizim
- ❖ Qalqilya
- ❖ Jenin

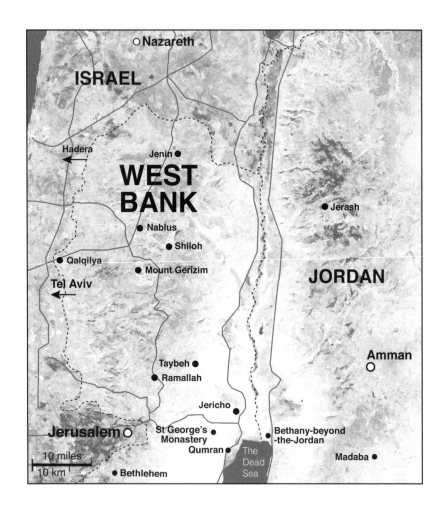

Introduction

The West Bank has borne the brunt of the Arab-Israeli conflict over the past half-century and continues to suffer the fallout from Israel's settlement programme and stranglehold on the local economy. In the past, it has often been in the media for the wrong reasons. Some Israelis and others will gasp in horror to hear that you are planning a visit to their neighbours. Yet this is, and has been for the past decade, a safe and fascinating part of the world, which is crying out for your attention—not least because of the large Christian minority who make up 20 per cent of Palestinians in the West Bank.

One of the issues for outsiders is to understand that, like everything else in this part of the world, there are more than two sides to every issue and situation. This is the other side to the story of the Israeli security wall and the region's impassioned politics. The West Bank is also a thriving, friendly place where you can very quickly and easily interact with local people and learn much about the history and politics of this land. You will be greeted with nothing but warmth and hospitality, should you choose to spend a few days among a community, both Muslim and Christian, that sometimes seems forgotten by the outside world.

It's easy to get off the beaten track and check out tiny Christian villages and biblical sites almost devoid of visitors. The West Bank is the land where the Samaritans (not Muslim, Jewish or Christian) continue to live separately from their neighbours; where shopkeepers-turned-militants-turned-shopkeepers once more will willingly talk to you over coffee in what was once the besieged city of Nablus; where the arid plains of southern Israel feel far away from the vineyards, olive groves and streams of the gently rolling hills.

The contemporary history and politics of the place also never seem far away. Whether you are touring a brewery overlooking a beautiful green valley, visiting one of the refugee camps that have become established suburbs of all the main cities and towns, looking out across the Jordan

Valley from the heights above Jericho or walking around the only zoo in Palestine, you are always likely to hear the views of your hosts as you gain insight into the daily life of ordinary Palestinians.

The Palestinian people are an educated, open-minded lot who have worked very hard in recent years to make the best of their situation, despite the countless issues that affect everything from their economy to the very existence of their state and government. One example is the security wall. While it is undoubtedly a huge intrusion into the West Bank and a clear violation of the Palestinians' human rights (not to mention international law), the wall has made Israel—and the West Bank—safer. The Palestinian Territories' current eight per cent annual economic growth rate has come off the back of this increase in stability and safety, and you will find Palestinians arguing in favour of the wall because of the economic stability and increased tourism that it has helped to bring.

At the same time, the way the Israeli government has continually stolen land and precious water resources from the West Bank for its own population has had a hugely detrimental impact on ordinary Palestinians. With a stalled peace process and the increased influence of the Orthodox and other right-wing parties in the Israeli parliament, positive steps towards a lasting political settlement (the full two-state solution favoured by most of the international community) seem as far away as ever. Israel may be the only mature democracy in the Middle East, but the Palestinians value democracy too. Even with 800,000 of their population living in internal refugee camps, they have the highest literacy rates in the entire Arab world, including the Gulf, and women here get a far better deal than in many neighbouring countries.

Of course, it's best to see this complex situation for yourself before making your mind up about where you stand. For the pilgrim, though, the West Bank is an essential destination and visitors should not feel nervous about crossing Israel's security wall and discovering what lies on the other side. Tourism is an essential part of the Palestinian economy and your money will have a big and lasting impact here. The area hugely rewards the effort of seeking it out and getting around either independently or as a member of a local tour. It can also be covered in day trips from Jerusalem or by staying a few nights locally, allowing the biblical sites in both the northern and the southern halves of the territory to be experienced, often without many fellow tourists, if any, in tow.

Bethlehem is the one tourist honeypot, and more than 90 per cent of incoming visitors to the West Bank only visit this town, normally as a day trip from Jerusalem. It would be greatly beneficial to locals if Western tourists began to stay in the town in large numbers, but even without the overnight stays, Bethlehem is experiencing an uplift in visitor numbers and the centre of town is thriving. With a university and cultural scene too, it deserves to be on the map in its own right, not just for being the birthplace of Jesus—but definitely for that reason too!

Down in Hebron, the continued friction between Jewish settlers and local Arabs, and the importance of the city of Abraham to all three faiths, has long sustained tensions that have ruined trade in the Old City and created an uneasy situation on the ground. The locals are still welcoming, however, and Hebron remains, at the time of writing, a fascinating and safe city to visit.

North, in Ramallah and Nablus, there are further settler tensions, with few if any tourists to help boost the local economy or report back on what the situation is really like. This is a great pity, since both cities and the surrounding areas are key destinations. In the villages up and down the West Bank, you can find enormous hospitality and a people who will be delighted to see you, speak with you and show you around.

Accessing the West Bank from Israel is currently a relaxed experience compared with the chaos of the past, and Westerners will have few difficulties, if any, at the border crossings. If you wish to engage with local tour guides, the Alternative Tourism Group (www.atg.ps) offers the widest range of services and welcomes those who are open to becoming what it calls 'transformational pilgrims' to Palestine. This Christian company includes the friendly and knowledgeable Sami and Mohanned as principal guides, who run day and half-day trips and are also available to put together tailored itineraries at very reasonable cost. They can also arrange homestays in Christian villages such as Beit Sahour near Bethlehem and can introduce you to a wide range of Arab Christian groups, businesses and politicians, should you express an interest in meeting them.

The Israel-based Green Olive Tours is another excellent value-for-money operation, which works with groups such as ATG to promote tourism in the West Bank as well as offering comprehensive tours of Israel itself. Whether you are travelling completely alone or as a family or church group, Green Olive's expertise and ability to offer tailored tours based on your own needs and interests is second to none. Manager Fred Schlomka is a bit of a legend when it comes to Israeli and Palestinian tourism initiatives and has been at the forefront of promoting understanding not just among tourists but among Israelis, too, for many years.

Finally, the 'soldiers for peace' programme Breaking the Silence is worthy of your support and can give a truly unique insight into both the settler and security situation in Hebron and the southern West Bank. This is a non-profit organisation set up by ex-IDF combatants principally to show fellow Israelis and others the truth behind the Israeli military intervention in the West Bank.

Check them out at www.breakingthesilence.org.il.

Footsteps

After several days in the West Bank as a guest of some of the guides mentioned here (ATG, Green Olive and Breaking the Silence), I had heard a lot about how everyday Palestinian life was routinely disrupted by the actions of the IDF. Especially enlightening was the way ex-IDF soldiers themselves explained how Israel's armed forces are used as a tool to control and subjugate a civilian population— often for the benefit of, and in the name of protecting, the settler community. Walking around the alleyways of Hebron and witnessing for myself the abuse dished out to ordinary Palestinian schoolchildren and women by the settler community was a real eye-opener. It was not that the settlers discriminated only against Palestinians; they were just as happy to mete out abuse to tourists and their own fellow Israelis as to their Palestinian neighbours.

Suffice to say that settlers and right-wing Israelis did not come off very well on any of the tours I participated in. In fact, the disproportionately negative effect of the settlers on the Arab-Israeli situation and, therefore, the entire region and rest of the world is utterly depressing. In Hebron alone it takes a permanent deployment of over 4000 heavily armed IDF soldiers to 'protect' fewer than 400

Jewish settlers, who regularly set out to disrupt and terrorise the Palestinians around them.

Unperturbed, and in the interests of balanced reporting for this book, I attempted to approach the settler community both in person (at the Tel Rumeida settlement in Hebron) and through open forums on the internet, to try to understand their religious and political reasons for pursuing their particular agenda of settling in Palestinian territory. Both attempts failed miserably and led to accusations of bias, at first because I was a Westerner and even more so when I explained that I was a Christian writer. Any attempt to engage openly about why settlers are in the West Bank in the first place, or to ask about settler–Palestinian dialogue, was met not with rebuttal or historical or religious discussion, but with extreme abuse.

Based on my own experience, I would say that it's not just racism and bigotry that fuel the settler community; it seems to be outright hatred for anyone different in any way from themselves. My only successful engagement with the community came about by catching the settler bus (Egged service 160) from Jerusalem central bus station to Hebron and talking with my neighbour Yachob. Although initially friendly and much more measured than some of his settler brothers, he was still highly suspicious of my motivations, simply because I was Western and Christian. Talking to him made me feel depressed about the situation.

It's pretty obvious to me, as an outsider with some understanding of both the Israeli and Palestinian causes, that the settler community in the West Bank is wreaking havoc with the peace process and causing massive social, political, environmental and economic damage to all sides. Why, then, have successive Israeli governments, from all political parties, allowed settlements to be built in the first place? The simple answer to this question is 'votes'. The settlers and their supporters in both the right-wing and Orthodox political parties make up a very important political bloc, which few Israeli politicians are brave enough to challenge. The recent fragmentation of Israeli politics into ever more minority parties has unfortunately handed the settlers a disproportionate and growing political influence, which they aggressively manipulate for their own ends.

For the time being, there seems to be no workable solution.

There are various discussion points on the web on both sides of the situation. For a more nuanced and objective view of the settler issue, look to one of the more academic texts mentioned in the Bibliography.

Bethlehem

Built across a number of steep hills and valleys, Bethlehem resembles Jerusalem at times, especially in terms of urban sprawl. If you're imagining a quaint little village surrounded by fields and green hillsides, today's city will make you think again. Almost a suburb of southern Jerusalem, Bethlehem has grown rapidly in recent decades and is now the largest centre for Arab Christians in the Middle East, with a population of 40,000. The city has succeeded in building a reputation for good inter-community relations. As in much of the West Bank, Christians and Muslims live here side by side and, while issues do arise, in general there are more factors that unite the two communities than divide them. Of course, today the city attracts many thousands of Christian pilgrims every day. It's not quite up to Mecca proportions, however, and this is the standard joke among Muslim taxi drivers ferrying you to the sites.

'But you, Bethlehem, in the land of Judah, are by no means least among the rulers of Judah; for out of you will come a ruler who will shepherd my people Israel.'

Matthew 2:6–7

Even with a fleeting visit to the city, the thing that people will notice and wish to talk about more than any other contemporary issue is undoubtedly the security wall. This is also a must-see part of any visit to Bethlehem: a walk along the concrete will allow you to witness for yourself the impact of this intimidating structure, with its countless watch towers, complete with blacked-out windows and heavily armed checkpoints. A lot of the graffiti along the wall belongs to international visitors who have chosen to record their take on the Palestinian situation. Banksy is perhaps the most famous of these artistic narrators, although other artists have left their mark here, too, such as Ron English and Swoon. The section of wall that runs along the main road leading into Aida refugee camp is full of references to the Palestinians' struggle (both armed and peaceful) against the wall itself and against Israeli military incursions into Palestinian territory.

Footsteps

The atmosphere inside the Aida refugee camp is remarkably relaxed, considering that over 3000 people are crammed into an area just one-tenth of a square kilometre. If you walk through slowly, the local children will come out first, but not long after they've called out their hellos, the adults will begin to follow.

Dan, aged 20, tells me he's just been let out of an Israeli prison.

His crime? He refused to say—his eyes shaded darkly by enormous bags, as if he hadn't slept in weeks. All he wanted now, he said, was the opportunity to work, earn some money and look after his family.

Further into the maze of alleyways at the heart of the camp, the rhythm of life is revealed through the closeness of the buildings. The noise from one household is easily carried across an entire block where as many as 20 or 30 houses may be built on top of one another, all with their windows and doors open to the afternoon heat.

Back at the entrance to Aida, the wall is completely covered by artwork. There are guns, masked figures and slogans in both Arabic and English. Some of the most famous of Banksy's murals depict a girl frisking a soldier and an IDF member checking a donkey's ID papers. There are several more Banksy murals in Bethlehem: a walk along the stretch of wall around Derech Hevron Road will reveal many hundreds of pieces of art with slogans ranging from 'Make hummus not walls' to 'This Lie cannot stand'.

If you have been able to catch the local Arab No. 21 bus from outside Jaffa Gate in Jerusalem (the bus originates from the bus station just to the north of Damascus Gate), the Bethlehem bus stop is a 15-minute walk from the Church of the Nativity. You can then walk through the heart of Bethlehem, the city centre, with its many shops and cafés thronging the streets and alleyways.

You can make the journey by hiring a local taxi to bring you directly into Manger Square: expect to pay around 20 NIS to be transported from the Arab side of the checkpoint, or take the opportunity to see other sites, such as the Shepherds' Fields, on the way. Add another 50 NIS for the taxi back towards the Old City once you've crossed back on to the Israeli side. It's probably easier (as well as much cheaper) to catch the bus if you only wish to see Manger Square.

The Church of the Nativity

Just like the Church of the Holy Sepulchre, the Church of the Nativity is a great survivor. First consecrated by Constantine in 326, it is the oldest church in the world and has been in continuous use for nearly 1700 years. The church has managed this longevity by constantly adapting to its environment, both political and physical. It has come through several earthquakes and military incursions, having been ruled by the British, the Ottomans, the Mamluks, the Romans and the Crusaders. The great red and black columns down either side of the nave are some of the most obvious original elements, as are the lower exterior walls, although much of the structure was rebuilt in the sixth century after a devastating fire.

The main entrance, the Door of Humility, illustrates some of those changes: the outline of the medieval door was bricked in during the late Crusader period to create a much smaller entrance, which remains in use today. Be prepared to duck! The grotto or cave on which the church was built is akin to the one in the Church of the Holy Sepulchre in terms of authenticity. As you go down the steps, you will see a small altar with a gold star set in the rock underneath it. This site has been identified as the birthplace of Jesus since at least AD135, and was traditionally identified (but with no written record) immediately after Jesus' death. Justin Martyr identifies the site in his writings of the early second century, and we are all familiar with the Bible readings.

So Joseph also went up from the town of Nazareth in Galilee to Judea, to Bethlehem the town of David, because he belonged to the house and line of David. He went there to register with Mary, who was pledged to be married to him and was expecting a child. While they were there, the time came for the baby to be born, and she gave birth to her firstborn, a son. She wrapped him in cloths and placed him in a manger, because there was no guest room available for them.

LUKE 2:4–7

Next door to the church is another, newer building, St Catherine's Catholic Church, which, with its cloisters and more light-filled architecture, is a more modern place to explore. Just like the Church of the Nativity, it will be packed out from mid-morning onwards. The best way to avoid the queues is to stay overnight in Bethlehem and visit early in the morning or from around 4.00 pm onwards, when all of the daytrippers and coach tour parties will have left. Having the place to yourself, finding time to sit quietly next to the grotto without being shoved out of the way by an over-zealous priest or camera-toting pilgrim, will make for a much more meaningful experience than you will get at midday. Not everyone will have this luxury but, even if you do come out on a day trip from Jerusalem, try your very best to be here at around 8.00 am.

The Church of the Nativity hit the headlines after the siege by the IDF in April 2002. The Israelis made a large-scale incursion into Bethlehem, intent on arresting several dozen Palestinian militants, who reacted by taking refuge inside the church. After much international diplomatic effort and pressure, including a delegation sent direct from the Vatican and a British Army negotiating team, the siege eventually came to an end in mid-May. By then, eight Palestinians had been killed, one Franciscan monk wounded and superficial damage caused to the church.

Since that low point, tourism has increased year on year, and today Manger Square is not just at peace but buzzing. The high-pressure hawking that was commonplace even five years ago seems to have vanished and you can now walk freely around the shops, streets and alleyways without any hassle. The Stars and Bucks coffee shop and café on the ground floor of the Peace Centre (which has good-quality public toilets in the basement) can refresh you after hours spent walking through the city centre and around the church. The church is open every day from 6.30 am to 7.30 pm.

Shepherds' Fields

Just south of Manger Square, along Shepherds' Road, is the site where the angel revealed to the shepherds that a Saviour had been born in the nearby town and was lying in a manger. Today's site consists of a small Franciscan chapel inside a cave cut into the hillside, the Church of the Angels and markers around the field. There is another location associated with the shepherds further out of town, but this is certainly the busiest and most established of the two. Inside the chapel, designed by Italian architect Antonio Barluzzi (see pages 147–148), there is an impressive bronze angel above the door. The paintings on the walls by the altar sum up the atmosphere of that first Christmas night.

A taxi from Manger Square will take you out to the site, which, with Herodian, makes a convenient round trip from the centre of town. The Fields are open from 8.00 am to 6.00

pm every day. Expect to pay a taxi around 20 NIS each way, or at least 50 NIS to take you and wait for half an hour or so at a time, while you explore each site. If you have negotiated a taxi for a half or full day, you may wish to see these locations before heading further south, to Hebron, for example.

And there were shepherds living out in the fields near by, keeping watch over their flocks at night. An angel of the Lord appeared to them, and the glory of the Lord shone around them, and they were terrified. But the angel said to them, 'Do not be afraid. I bring you good news that will cause great joy for all the people. Today in the town of David a Saviour has been born to you; he is the Messiah, the Lord. This will be a sign to you: you will find a baby wrapped in cloths and lying in a manger.'

Luke 2:8–12

Herodian

Unmissable from miles around, just as it was always intended to be, the hilltop acropolis of Herodian is still slowly revealing itself. Despite being sacked in the first century, the remains of Herod's tomb itself were found there by archaeologists in 2007. Today, these works are still ongoing to explore one of the wonders of the ancient Middle East. Clearly, the site has a lot to show and tell about life for the Roman élite at the time of Jesus, and it is best discovered by taking a self-guided tour on foot. The site is especially busy on Fridays, when Israeli school groups like to head over. Note that there is no public transport out here, so unless you come as part of a tour the best option is to hire a taxi in Bethlehem and get the driver to wait for you at Herodian. As already mentioned, the best value can be gained by combining visits to Herodian and

Shepherds' Fields before returning into town or venturing further into the southern half of the West Bank. The site is open every day from 9.00 am to 5.30 pm, except on *Shabbat*, when it closes at 12.30 pm.

Hebron

About 45 minutes south of Bethlehem lies the city of Hebron, one of the most historic (and holy) places in this part of the world—which is really saying something, considering everything else that is in the area. As the final resting place of Abraham, father of all three monotheistic faiths, Hebron should be right at the top of most people's travel itineraries. The fact that it's often overlooked is down to some bad publicity dating mainly to the first and second *intifadas*, when the city was one of the epicentres of Palestinian resistance to the Israeli occupation, and military incursions into the city by the IDF were common. No place brings the Arab-Israeli situation so immediately to life than this one. Not only is it the city of Abraham, but it is also the only place on earth where a mosque and synagogue share the same space and Jews and Muslims pray and worship (almost) side by side.

So far, so intriguing. Unfortunately, this relationship has regularly been at the heart of violence and counter-violence from both sides. The area's traditionally small Jewish community was bolstered in the 1980s by a wave of new settlers, many of them recent immigrants to Israel who were politically or religiously motivated to reclaim Hebron for themselves. Current tensions date back to 1994, when Baruch Goldstein, a local Israeli settler who liked to wear a Nazi-era 'Jude' yellow star on his clothes, took his reservist-issue automatic rifle into the mosque and murdered 29 Muslims as they prayed. He managed to wound more than 100 more people before the worshippers in the mosque overpowered him and beat him to death. The fighting in Hebron over the following weeks saw another 30 Palestinians killed and the city's reputation to the outside world tarnished. Pilgrimage to this most holy of sites became out of the question for most people.

This shocking event caused a meltdown in local Jewish–Muslim relations that still has repercussions today. Even though the Rabin government denounced Goldstein as a terrorist and ordered the IDF to bulldoze his grave, his actions destroyed local dialogue between Jews and Arabs. With 400 Israeli settlers living in the centre of the Old City in order to be close to the Tomb of the Patriarchs, it can seem that their wishes override those of the 130,000 Muslims and 10,000 Christians also present in the city. Is it any wonder that the Arab community here is still so angry?

It seems crazy to an outsider that this situation has developed. Nowhere is the Israeli policy of allowing Jewish settlers (almost) free rein to live anywhere they wish in the West Bank so discredited. Above all else, the settlers and the government simply seem to lack all common sense, especially as it takes 4000 IDF troops to protect the settlers round the clock. If you get the chance to walk along the alleyways of the old city, you will see for yourself the places where settlers have made a pastime out of provoking their Arab neighbours by pouring acid, rubbish and sewage on to the streets below their windows.

All this, understandably, has had a devastating effect on the amount of tourism that flows through the city, which is a huge shame, because Hebron has a beautiful Old City and the Abraham/Ibrahim tomb is at the centre of the attractions. As a tourist, you will be in the privileged position of being able to visit both the synagogue and the mosque and view the tombs of the patriarchs from both sides of the building. Inside the mosque, where visitors are free to walk around (although women will need to put on a large Ottoman-style white shawl), you can hear the singing in the synagogue on the other side of the internal wall while sitting down to pray. On the synagogue side, the rooms are often packed with Orthodox believers, swaying and singing in beautiful harmony.

Footsteps

From the street below the entrance to the Abraham synagogue, it was the song that first grabbed my attention. It was a hot day, the kind that beats you over the head and forces you to seek shade as quickly as you can, and I was glad of the cover of the building and the friendly welcome by the young IDF guards. But it was definitely the melodious singing that had caught my imagination. Heading up the steps to the first anteroom of the synagogue, I found perhaps 100 Orthodox Jewish men singing at the tops of their voices. The effect was mesmerising and those of us at the back of the room just stood open-mouthed in awe and humility.

On the Ibrahimi mosque side of the room, I removed my shoes and joined the Imam in a quick prayer at the foot of Abraham's tomb itself, which was draped in a green and gold cover and was visible through an iron grate. A small niche on the right-hand side of the grate contains a footprint said to belong to Mohammed himself. On the other side of the tomb, through an identical iron grate, is the synagogue. How close the two faiths are, and yet so intractably apart in the eyes of so many, is the real issue of the day here. Few seem interested in building dialogue and promoting peace, apart from NGOs, including charities such as Christian Aid, who have a long-standing presence in the West Bank.

It is easy to be cynical about the effects of tourism, but we should talk to organisations such as Green Olive and Breaking the Silence before judging. These tour operators are committed first and foremost to engagement with all communities, exposing tourists to those communities and their views. Their motivation is not to make money, and their work is not without risk, both personal and political, but they are committed to opening outsiders' eyes to the reality of life on the ground here. They are among the many people inside Israel who are brave enough to put their heads above the parapet and say, 'Look at the truth here', even when it means being demonised by other members of their own community. (See the pro-Zionist www.ngo-monitor.org for the alternative view of these and other organisations and charities working in both Israel and the Palestinian territories.)

Ultimately, the more Christian pilgrims who continue to engage with these organisations on their tours and talk about these situations when they return home, the better the chance of promoting peace at all levels. For that reason alone, long may their work continue.

Hebron is undoubtedly one of the most important shrines for Jews, Muslims and Christians. In this place, to an outsider, the close relationship between all of our religions is so obvious that the essential crux of conflict in the Holy Land seems more akin to a family feud than an insurmountable geo-political problem. The danger with the latter view is that it makes interest and intervention too difficult, especially when it is the former reading of the situation that makes the most sense. On the streets of Hebron, this truth comes home to rest.

Founded in 1730BC, Hebron is one of the oldest cities in the world and was built upon a key trading route between the Mediterranean and the Arabian peninsula. Canaanite tribes settled the first villages here and Jews established themselves several centuries before Jesus. The Canaanites and later the Arabs accepted this situation, and there has been continuous settlement of both Jews and Arabs here since then. In more recent times, the small Jewish community has remained committed, alongside its Muslim neighbours, to commemorating the resting place of the patriarchs of all three monotheistic religions—Abraham, Isaac and Jacob—and their wives. Muslims also believe that Hebron was the place where Adam and Eve settled in exile and worked the earth after being banished from the garden of Eden. The patriarchs (immediate descendants of Abraham) were buried at Hebron from around 2000BC, after Abraham had bought a field and cave near the centre of the settlement, which was then just a village. This is the site of today's synagogue/mosque.

And the Lord God said, 'The man has now become like one of us, knowing good and evil. He must not be allowed to reach out his hand and take also from the tree of life and eat, and live for ever.' So the Lord God banished him from the Garden of Eden to work the ground from which he had been taken. After he drove the man out, he placed on the east side of the Garden of Eden cherubim and a flaming sword flashing back and forth to guard the way to the tree of life.

GENESIS 3:22–24

Getting to and from Hebron is best done by taxi from Bethlehem, on an organised tour, or on the Egged bus from Jerusalem (see below). A visit to one of the glass and ceramic factories on the outskirts of the old city at Jerusalem Square is often included in tours, and provides some good souvenir-buying opportunities. This part of the city (very much the commercial centre) also has some good, cheap restaurants and cafés in which you will be made very welcome. There's also an opportunity to buy authentic Jordanian (red) and Palestinian (black) chequered scarves, or *keffiyeh*, made famous by Yasser Arafat.

The last Palestinian factory making black *keffiyeh* is in Hebron (in the past two decades, the trade has largely been overwhelmed by cheap Chinese imports). Ask a taxi driver to take you to visit the Herbawi textile factory, or buy an authentic Herbawi scarf from one of the Palestinian shops around Jerusalem Square. Back in town, the souq around Tel Rumeida is a traditional Ottoman warren of alleyways and shops, selling everything from food to furniture. The presence of the settlers above the Tel Rumeida district will be discussed by your guide, or the situation may reveal itself to you while you walk alone through the alleys with the ever-intimidating presence of wire mesh above your head to keep out the largest of the settlers' projectiles.

Staying the night and walking around the old city after dark will give you yet another perspective on Hebron. Taxis run until late, but if you wish to head back to Jerusalem, remember that although the Bethlehem checkpoint is supposedly open 24 hours a day, it is always best to double check and ask locals about its current status. There are few hotels in Hebron itself to choose from, although the Royal Suites hotel on Nimra Street has huge rooms with a *mezze* (buffet) breakfast from around £30 per night. Alternatively, ask your guide or tour company to help you make contact with Christian homestays in the area: local group ATG can again advise or arrange accommodation on your behalf.

To gain a different perspective on Hebron, you can also travel to the city on the No. 160 Egged bus from Jerusalem central bus station. This bus is usually used only by the settler community. People may be returning home after visiting the capital and a conversation with your neighbour may be more informative and insightful than you expect: not all settlers sound like right-wing extremists. The bus also stops very conveniently next to the Tomb of the Patriarchs/Ibrahimi mosque, and is the cheapest way to travel independently to the city, at 10 NIS each way for the one-hour journey. Buses run every half hour from early morning until 11 pm.

Ramallah

The capital of the Palestinian Authority, Ramallah is a bustling city just north of Jerusalem, on the No. 18 bus route from the Damascus Gate bus station and just beyond the northern terminus of Jerusalem's tram. No location in the northern West Bank is far from here, so it also makes a good base as well as a destination in itself—not least to see Arafat's amazing white marble tomb and to wander through one of the most bustling souqs and shopping areas in the region.

Any bus or taxi service into Ramallah will drop you just a two-minute walk east of Lions' Square (Al-Manara), which is the very heart of the city. Continuing west on Al-Raesey will eventually bring you to the ill-defined old city: walking downhill, look for the minaret of a mosque and tower of a church close to one another. To get from Lions' Square to Arafat's tomb, walk north for 15–20 minutes until the white perimeter walls of the Palestinian Authority compound become visible. Entrance to the tomb is on the northern (right-hand) side of the compound as you walk from the city centre. It's common to have the place to yourself, with the dazzling white marble plaza blinding on a sunny day. Photographs are allowed and the ceremonial guards are usually friendly and more than willing to pose for a photo with you.

Despite recent changes, Western tourists are still in short supply here and people from all walks of life, from soldiers and taxi drivers to shopkeepers and academics, will want to engage with you and use their English, which is taught in all Palestinian schools. Again, there will be no shortage of opportunity to discuss the Arab-Israeli situation and talk about the many different routes to building a sustainable peace settlement. People love to talk about the issue and, whether you are interested or not, you will soon find yourself in conversation about it. Most of all, Palestinians are always keen to hear what you think about the situation, especially as a Christian.

Taybeh

Ten miles north-east of Ramallah is Taybeh, one of the very few Christian-majority towns in the West Bank and home to a continuous Christian population since the third century. Possibly named in the Bible as the village of Ephraim, this may be the place where Jesus and the disciples spent a night or two on their way to Bethany before entering Jerusalem for the last time.

Therefore Jesus no longer moved about publicly among the people
of Judea. Instead he withdrew to a region near the wilderness,
to a village called Ephraim, where he stayed with his disciples.
JOHN 11:54

Today, the highlight of the town is without doubt the Taybeh
brewery, where the Khoury family have been making Palestine's finest (and only!) beer for 20 years. Head brewer Nadim
Khoury runs free 30-minute tours throughout the day. Made
in accordance with the German purity laws of 1516 (which
permitted only hops, barley and water to be used to brew
beer), the range of beers has expanded since the brewery's
foundation but the focus is on three main drinks—a German-
style lager, a dark ale and a honey-coloured amber. The
Khoury family's future plans include building an 80-room
hotel to help keep the town on the map, and to start producing the first Palestinian wine.

Establishing a year-round tourist trade is firmly on the
agenda here, especially during the brewery's very own Okto-
berfest, usually run on the first weekend of October in both
Taybeh and Ramallah. Given the town's importance as a site
of Christian pilgrimage, this should be, again, a major destination on many people's travel itinerary. Despite its location
in the Judean hills, it is not far from Jerusalem (less than 20
miles) and should take no more than an hour to reach, or
less if arranged through an organised tour. If you are visiting
by taxi, one option is to include a stop in Taybeh on the way
to Jericho from Ramallah or vice versa.

There are three active churches in the centre of the town—a
Latin (Catholic) church, an Orthodox church (built in 1931)
and a Greek-Melkite church. In town are also the ruins of two
Byzantine churches, including the impressive wall of the El-

Kheder church behind the Melkite one. The French Sisters of the Cross run a convent and pilgrim house. Bookings can be made by phone (+972 2 289 8161) or by emailing scjtaybe@palnet.com. Rooms start at £30 per person per night.

A taxi ride to Taybeh from Ramallah should cost no more than 50 NIS, but be careful to ensure that you can get back again afterwards. There are only one or two buses per hour passing this way (they take about 40 minutes to reach Ramallah's central bus station and cost 6 NIS) and taxis can be hard to find, especially from the middle of the afternoon onwards. The town council runs a useful English-language website at www.taybeh.info/en.

Nablus

The largest of the northern West Bank cities, Nablus is in a dramatic setting between two steep mountains with modern high-rise buildings clinging to the valley sides. The vibe is very different from Hebron or Ramallah. Nablus is more modern and yet somehow more traditional at the same time. There is clearly a large amount of investment being made here, with lots of construction projects and new roads taking shape. Yet a walk through the city centre will reveal reminders of its role as the focus of both of the Palestinian *intifadas*. Many hundreds if not thousands of local people died here in previous decades, and posters and murals glorifying local fighters adorn the city's streets, much like the Shankill and Falls Road areas of Belfast.

The bustling old souq remains the heart of the city and can easily take up an hour or more of your time, as you can see and buy everything here, from falafel sandwiches to whole camel heads at the local butchers. The Ottoman-era arcades are typically small and narrow, and good shoes will be essential to avoid some of the more exotic detritus from the local butchers and food shops. The smells and sights are sometimes shocking, sometimes surprising, but you will definitely find that shopkeepers and other locals make many attempts to talk and invite you for a coffee. A Western tourist in town is still relatively unusual and you are likely to be a magnet for children and others intent on practising their English language skills. It's a friendly place which is also an excellent base for venturing out to nearby Qalqilya, Mount Gerizim, Jenin or Shiloh. The many olive-oil soap factories offer another different insight into the local community and economy. The Mofthen factory on Martyr's Square, at the front of the entrance to the souq, is the easiest to find.

On the eastern edge of Nablus is Jacob's Well Church, with its famous watering hole—completed only in 2001, although the building appears much older. It is built over other ancient churches and basilicas dating back to the Byzantine era. The well itself is said to date from the time of Jesus, while the main structure is from 1860. The roof and tower are the parts that were completed at the beginning of the 21st century: photos inside reveal the construction process in more detail. Look out for the guide who will happily show you the well in the basement and tell you more about its biblical history and recite chapter and verse from the Bible. You can drop a cupful of water from the mouth of the well and wait more than 30 seconds before you hear it hit the bottom—very spooky! The church and its well are said to be on the spot where Jesus stopped a Samaritan woman and asked her for a drink of water:

Now Jesus learned that the Pharisees had heard that he was gaining and baptising more disciples than John—although in fact it was not Jesus who baptised, but his disciples. So he left Judea and went back once more to Galilee. Now he had to go through Samaria. So he came to a town in Samaria called Sychar, near the plot of ground Jacob had given to his son Joseph. Jacob's well was there, and Jesus, tired as he was from the journey, sat down by the well. It was about noon. When a Samaritan woman came to draw water, Jesus said to her, 'Will you give me a drink?' (His disciples had gone into the town to buy food.) The Samaritan woman said to him, 'You are a Jew and I am a Samaritan woman. How can you ask me for a drink?' (For Jews do not associate with Samaritans.) Jesus answered her, 'If you knew the gift of God and who it is that asks you for a drink, you would have asked him and he would have given you living water.'

JOHN 4:1–10

On the opposite side of the main road from Jacob's Well Church is the Batata refugee camp, with its active Women's Centre managed by Ibtesam Mizhar. She will happily chat to you about the challenges of promoting women's rights and healthcare within Palestine, and it is heartening to witness at first hand the remarkable work being done here to promote equality of opportunity, childcare, education and cultural initiatives for refugees. While talking with those running the centre, you will be reminded of some of the Palestinians' strengths as a people and a nation. Education here is among the best in the Arab world, with near-universal literacy even in places like Batata. Visitors are welcome to find out more, walk around the centre and even take part in the initiatives themselves. If you have a particular business skill or insight into the church, and there is an English-speaking group in attendance, Ibtesam and her colleagues will be happy to allow you to talk to them. There is also a small shop selling goods from the women's cooperative, such as scarves and jewellery, alongside other crafts and Palestinian-sourced food. Please consider buying some souvenirs here in order to support the centre and its attendees financially as well as symbolically by your visit.

Mount Gerizim

The presence of the tiny Samaritan community of Kiryat Luza upon Mount Gerizim offers a fascinating insight into one of the most remarkable communities in the Middle East. Followers of neither Christianity, Islam nor Judaism, Samaritans follow their own scripture and use a language closely derived from ancient Hebrew and Aramaic. While the Samaritan faith is closest to Judaism in terms of doctrine and tradition, the community has always remained resolutely independent and is loyal to its ancient land in the middle of the West Bank. The Hebrew-style alphabet may look familiar but is in fact unique, and the community is rightly proud of its efforts to preserve one of the oldest and least-dominant languages, cultures and faiths on earth.

Said to be descendents of Joseph, the son of Jacob, and thus related to the first tribes of Israel, the Samaritans once numbered more than a million people, although today the numbers have decreased to an unsustainable couple of thousand. The only other Samaritan community is located at Holon, near Tel Aviv.

Due to the very small size of the community, on a visit to Kiryat Luza you may be surprised to see recent Eastern European migrants (all women) walking round town in short skirts and revealing tops. These young women have been encouraged to settle here to address the low birth rate. So far, the policy has been moderately successful, so we can expect to see more young women moving into the community in the future. The initiative does, however, dilute the Samaritan bloodline, so future generations of Samaritans may have an even more complex genealogy than they have already. This somewhat surprising reality is just one of many unusual and unexpected parts of the culture.

At the same time, being a tiny island of difference (just 800 people at the last census) has not been easy, and the gates on the approach roads are a reminder that even now, in days of relative peace and harmony, the community prefers to go into self-imposed curfew at nightfall, when the barriers come down and driving through town is impossible for outsiders. There are few shops and amenities in the town itself, with the focus being on family life and worship.

The essential stop for any visitor to Kiryat Luza is the visitor centre, which doubles up as the world's only Samaritan museum and is next door to the fascinating Samaritan temple. The elderly gentleman who welcomes visitors to the centre on most days is Husney Cohen, one of the Samaritans' high priests. His broken English can sometimes be hard to follow, but he is happy to talk and explain the history of his people to visitors and is a wonderful source of knowledge. Please don't miss out on the opportunity to hear direct from one of the community's leaders.

The remains of a fifth-century BC temple on the very summit of Mount Gerizim, overlooking Nablus, gives views as far as the River Jordan in the distance. Be careful when navigating old barbed wire fences and rocky outcrops as you scramble across the summit and around the stone floors of what remains of the temple. While Judaism places the birth of the world and the site of Abraham's attempted sacrifice of Isaac at the Temple Mount in Jerusalem, Samaritans place these events, and more, here on the summit of their mountain. For them, this is the site of the garden of Eden and the only piece of land that survived the flood. The Samaritans' version of events certainly wins out in terms of height and view over the nearby region: it's a very impressive location and it is little wonder the Samaritans have always held on to this strategic and symbolic vantage-point.

Samaritans are, of course, famous for their role in one of the best-known passages in the New Testament—the parable of the good Samaritan. In Jesus' time, as today, Samaritans were a marginalised minority, often misunderstood by their immediate neighbours. The Samaritans were definitely 'others' in first-century Palestine, and part of the parable's radically anti-establishment message is that those whom society least expects to come good are often the ones who do, while establishment groups can end up being those who hypocritically 'pass by on the other side' when confronted with suffering. More than this, the good Samaritan story also reflects on the practical application of how to love God and to love your neighbour as yourself. Luke summarises these aspects of Jesus' teaching perfectly:

And behold, a lawyer stood up to put [Jesus] to the test, saying: 'Teacher, what shall I do to inherit eternal life?' He said to him: 'What is written in the Law? How do you read it?' And he answered: 'You shall love the Lord your God with all your heart and with all your soul and with all your strength and with all your mind, and your neighbour as yourself.' And he said to him: 'You have answered correctly; do this, and you will live.'

But he, desiring to justify himself, said to Jesus: 'And who is my neighbour?'

Jesus replied: 'A man was going down from Jerusalem to Jericho, and he fell among robbers, who stripped him and beat him and departed, leaving him half dead. Now by chance a priest was going down that road, and when he saw him he passed by on the other side. So likewise a Levite, when he came to the place and saw him, passed by on the other side. But a Samaritan, as he journeyed, came to where he was, and when he saw him, he had compassion. He went to him and bound up his wounds, pouring on oil and wine. Then he set him on his own animal and brought him to an inn and took care of him. And the next day he took out two denarii and gave them to the innkeeper, saying: "Take care of him, and whatever more you spend, I will repay you when I come back."

'Which of these three, do you think, proved to be a neighbour to the man who fell among the robbers?' He said: 'The one who showed him mercy.' And Jesus said to him: 'You go, and do likewise.'

Luke 10:25–37

A taxi from the centre of Nablus to Gerizim will cost about 20 NIS. Expect to pay around NIS 40 per hour waiting time if you want your driver to wait for you and then take you on to another part of the West Bank. The going rate for a half-day with a taxi driver should be about 200 NIS—more if your driver takes you on a long round-trip (Ramallah to Jenin and back, for example).

Qalqilya

A 20-minute taxi ride west from Nablus (expect to pay no more than 60 NIS) brings you to a town that is more famous for its animal than its human population. Qalqilya is home to the only zoo in Palestine. Bordered closely by the Israeli security wall, in years past the zoo has been on the literal front line of Israeli military excursions into this part of the West Bank, so the story of the zoo closely mirrors that of the West Bank itself. One of the zoo's most famous inhabitants, Roothi the giraffe, was killed by Israeli rocket fire in 2001, but can still be seen guarding the entrance to the zoo's museum thanks to the taxidermy skills of Dr Sami Khader.

Both the zoo and Dr Khader have been made famous by Amelia Thomas's book, *The Zoo on the Road to Nablus*. All this is due to the dedication and tenacity of Dr Khader, who has become an expert at improvisation: he even makes his own hypodermic needles to get round an Israeli ban on the import of veterinary equipment. He has developed excellent links with the two zoos in Israel, as well as the likes of Berlin Zoo and London Zoo, which have long supported him and have supplied the zoo with second-hand equipment.

Always positive and smiling, Dr Khader sums up the indefatigable nature of the Palestinian spirit. Through years or even decades of restrictions and difficulties, he has battled on in his vision to give Palestinian children an insight into a wider world and a day's relief from often tough home lives. Not that the zoo is a children's playground only: by its nature (not least, its small size) it gives everyone the chance to get very close to some of the most remarkable animals on earth. A general zoo, its collection is especially strong on birds of prey, primates and big cats.

Today the zoo is growing, with up to 80 coachloads of children, including schoolchildren from Israel, visiting every day. Dr Khader says:

My vision is for a zoo that is just as much educational as recreational and which will teach young people about the environment, sustainability and recycling as well as respect for other animals. It's also a place for people to work—there are 42 staff looking after 350 animals here, so it's a really important part of the local community and local economy.

Jenin

The Freedom Theatre at the Jenin refugee camp is an exciting example of peace efforts, even though its founder, the Palestinian-Israeli filmmaker, director and actor Juliano Mer-Khamis, was assassinated outside the theatre in April 2011. The theatre's aim of generating cultural resistance by creating opportunities for local people and connecting Jenin with other parts of the world has been a huge success, of which Mer-Khamis was and would be proud. The theatre has toured in France and the US and has also performed works, both original and established, in Israel as well as throughout the West Bank. The theatre always welcomes international guests and takes volunteers, often from the UK, who are willing to work on its programmes (visit www.thefreedomtheatre.org).

Jenin also makes a convenient crossing point into the West Bank from the bottom of the Galilee and vice versa. The Jalame checkpoint is ten miles south of Nazareth, or six miles south of Afula. A taxi service runs once a day at 8.00 am from both Israeli cities to Jenin through the checkpoint. On the way out of town southwards (the road to Nablus), look out for the hull of a Palestinian Airlines plane currently being used as a restaurant.

Further reading

Edward Platt, *The City of Abraham* (Picador, 2012).
William Dalrymple, *From The Holy Mountain* (Flamingo, 1998).
Mark Thomas, *Extreme Rambling: Walking Israel's separation barrier. For fun* (Ebury Press, 2012).

Clockwise from top: the new Jerusalem tram; Palestinian children in Hebron; Aida refugee camp in the West Bank; street scenes from the Old City of Jerusalem (posters and pomegranates)

VISIT
PALESTINE

Jerusalem Old City

Top: *twilight over the Old City*

Middle: *the Dome of the Rock*

Bottom: *dawn view from the Mount of Olives*

Jerusalem Old City

Top: prayers at the Western Wall
Middle: the garden of Gethsemane
Bottom: view of the Western Wall plaza

Jerusalem

Top: Yad Vashem

Middle: modern buildings on Jaffa Road (left); the grave of Oskar Schindler (right)

Bottom: walking along the city walls

Bethlehem

Top: Banksy's famous donkey mural

Middle: the Church of the Nativity

Bottom: Fred Schlomka from Green Olive Tours

Galilee

Top: Cana, site of Jesus' first miracle

Middle: Yardenit baptism site, River Jordan (left); the Cliffs of Arbel (right)

Bottom: the Church of the Beatitudes (left); the Sea of Galilee (right)

Mediterranean

Top: *Tel Aviv*

Middle: *the beautiful Baha'i gardens, Haifa*

Bottom: *sunset over the sea at Akko*

Top: *a view of Nablus and Batata refugee camp from Mount Gerizim*

Middle: *Roman mosaics at Zippori National Park (left); police line up against protestors at Damascus Gate, Jerusalem (right)*

Bottom: *a rally is watched by an Orthodox Jewish man*

–Chapter 5–

The Dead Sea

This is one of the richest regions in the world, in terms of its history and archaeology.

❖ Introduction
❖ Qumran
❖ The Dead Sea
❖ Masada
❖ Jordan Valley
❖ St George's Monastery
❖ Jericho
❖ Bethany

Introduction

Many rewards await those who make the short journey east and then south of Jerusalem, down (literally—it is the lowest place on earth) to the Dead Sea. The miles may be few, but the change in scenery and climate is dramatic. Part of the northern reaches of the Great Rift Valley (which also includes the Sea of Galilee and reaches south as far as Lake Victoria and Mozambique), the Dead Sea was connected to the Mediterranean until two million years ago. Since then it has been growing gradually hotter and smaller. Even in winter, the heat can be unbearable around the sea (temperatures approaching 50°C are not uncommon) and many visitors find themselves unable to wait to get back to the relative cool of Jerusalem, which is nearly 2000 feet higher in altitude. On a comfortable day in the city it can be absolutely baking down at the Dead Sea, with heatstroke a real issue for visitors. A walk up to Masada, which overlooks the Dead Sea, is a tough 45-minute ascent of over 1000 feet. Allow a minimum of two litres of water for the hike and wear appropriate footwear (in other words, hiking boots). Trainers or sandals really won't do.

A traditional bathe in the sea for an afternoon can be fun but is also very hot: an hour in the water may well be enough. For many people, though, the best part of a trip to the region will be visiting the historical sites that are directly related to events in the Bible and the sites where ancient scrolls of the Bible were discovered, such as Qumran. The area is also very beautiful in its rocky, desert-climate, sand-blown way, and just a couple of hours can be enough to get the enthusiasm of the most jaded traveller up and running again.

There are few opportunities to stay around the Dead Sea. There are high-end resort hotels at Ein Borek, which fill up mainly with Israeli tourists, especially at weekends, and some tired accommodation options at Jericho. Otherwise, there is very little development of any kind, which is why most visitors make do with a day trip. You can hire a car for the day, of course, or take public transport (the No. 421, 444 and 486 Egged buses drive along the western shore of the sea, with stops at Ein Borek, Ein Gedi and Masada), which will enable you to jump off at any of the major sites and hotels. If you hire an economy car, make sure it has air-conditioning: it will be almost impossible to drive here without it.

Qumran

Believed to have been founded by the Essenes shortly after the time of Jesus, Qumran shot to fame in 1948, after a local Bedouin shepherd found an old scroll in an earthenware jar there. Over 1000 scrolls and pieces of manuscript were subsequently discovered in the caves around Qumran, representing different books of the Bible along with other accounts of first-century Palestine. These parchments—written in Hebrew, Aramaic and Greek—and the scraps are now collectively known as the Dead Sea Scrolls and are on display in the impressive House of the Book at the Israel Museum in Jerusalem (see pages 69–70).

The Qumran visitors' centre is inside a national park, just off the main north–south Highway 90, and charges 20 NIS entry. It's open from 8.00 am to 5.00 pm every day except Saturdays, when it closes at 3.00 pm. There is a short multimedia presentation and information providing a potted history of both the discovery of the scrolls and the Essene community as it was at the time of Jesus. A walk around one of the caves where the scrolls were actually discovered illuminates the unlikeliness of the discovery: one of the most important archaeological finds ever made in the Middle East is also the story of a humble Bedouin shepherd boy going about his daily chores, searching for lost sheep.

The Dead Sea

To take a dip in the Dead Sea, you have to pay for entry to one of the commercial beach resorts at Ein Gedi, Biankini Beach, Mineral Beach or Ein Bokek. It's definitely worth having facilities—not just for getting changed but also for the provision of first aid and lifeguards, should you have any problems. The Dead Sea is a very remote place in which to fall ill, even if you just swallow a bit too much salt water (unlikely, since your gag reflex should stop you from swallowing any) or, worse, get water from the sea in your eyes (which can cause temporary blindness). The black sand with which people so readily cover their bodies is toxic and you need to be careful at all times in and around the water. The rocks can be very sharp and you will need waterproof, thick-soled sandals to help you get in and out of the water. Doing it barefoot will make you very unsteady.

The healing properties of the water are, of course, legendary, and for good reason: there are a plethora of health benefits from the sea, which have not been exaggerated. The water comprises nearly 30 per cent minerals—such as bromide and magnesium, as well as common salt—which ensures your ability to float. Cuts and abrasions will sting but also be healed, as will skin problems. In addition, being over 1000 feet below sea level means that the air contains ten per cent more oxygen than at sea level. This should make breathing easier and deeper and will be a boon to asthmatics.

You can camp for free at Ein Gedi national park and there are some great budget accommodation options along this part of the coast. Both the youth hostel and the field study centre are excellent and cheap. Expect to walk a couple of kilometres out from here to the shoreline: since 1948, the sea has receded from the shore by several metres every year. A plan to pipe seawater from the Mediterranean (details of the Med-Dead proposals can be found at www.meddead.org) to replenish the lake and generate hydroelectric power, as well as to provide a reliable water source to Israel, the West Bank and Jordan, has yet to come to fruiting, due partly to the £4.5 billion price tag. The project is viable, though, and may become essential in another couple of decades if the Dead Sea is to survive at all.

Masada

One of the most impressive sites in the Middle East is firmly entrenched in Jewish minds because of its amazing story. It was once an important Jewish military base perched atop a dramatic bluff, and over 1000 Jewish rebels took to the fortress after the Roman conquest of Jerusalem in AD70, refusing to surrender to the Romans even when an entire legion—over 20,000 heavily armed soldiers—surrounded Masada.

Eventually the Romans built a siege ramp (still visible today, although the path runs out to a car park and the road to Arad, a 40-mile one-way drive around the bottom of the Judean hills) and used a giant battering ram to break down the walls of the fortress. As the Roman invaders swarmed inside, however, they were met with nothing but silence. Those inside Masada had all chosen suicide over surrender. They had drawn lots to decide who would kill whom until a single man was left; his final act was to kill himself.

It's a wonderfully evocative place, especially at sunrise or sunset, when it can be busier than it is during the day. A hike and clamber over the summit ruins at any time will bring the story of Masada vividly to life. It was obviously a very impressive fortress, with palatial dwellings for the wealthy (including a swimming pool for Herod), a synagogue and storehouses with many months' worth of food in readiness. The deep underground reservoir survives (accessible by a series of more than 100 steps) and demonstrates the ingenuity of the engineers and architects of Masada.

It's easy to catch a sunrise tour here, although you should be prepared to leave Jerusalem at 3.00 am to make it. Organised bus tours start at around NIS 100. If you are making your own arrangements, note that the national park charges a entry fee of 30 NIS. You will need to walk a couple of kilometres from Highway 90 if you've taken the bus. The steep ascent to the summit can be undertaken in less than an hour on foot via the Snake Path, or you can catch the cable car, which makes the journey in just a few minutes and is a thrill in itself (75 NIS return, including national park entry fee). The map and brochure that come with the entry fee are good, but, for more detail, think about hiring the audio tour for a further 20 NIS). Masada is a moody and mesmerising location and a full day can be combined with an overnight stay in Ein Gedi (it's worth staying at Masada until sundown) to get a proper feel for this part of Israel.

Jordan Valley

One possible site for Jesus' baptism has been identified at Qasr al-Yahud, just below the Allenby Bridge border crossing between Israel and Jordan. Another has been identified at Bethany Beyond the Jordan (see page 214).

To get to Qasr al-Yahud, drive towards the Jordanian border and look for the brown signs on the right, about five kilometres before the border itself. A taxi from Jericho will cost you about 50 NIS for the return trip. There's quite a bit of interest here: the site includes wide marble steps descending into the Jordan, as well as ruins of both a Byzantine and a Crusader church overlooking the river. Pilgrims can sometimes be found being baptised in the water. Taking a picnic as well as a Bible is a nice way to spend a lunch time at the site, which can make a welcome contrast with the intense heat of the Dead Sea.

> *At that time Jesus came from Nazareth in Galilee and was baptised by John in the Jordan. Just as Jesus was coming up out of the water, he saw heaven being torn open and the Spirit descending on him like a dove. And a voice came from heaven: 'You are my Son, whom I love; with you I am well pleased.'*
> MARK 1:9–11

According to some, Qasr al-Yahud is the place where the Israelites crossed over the Jordan on their way back into Israel. It's also the place from which the prophet Elijah ascended to heaven.

Driving north from the road to the Jordanian border means joining Highway 90, which runs due north into the Galilee at Beit She'an. With the rise of the Judean hills to the west and the heat-haze shimmer of the Jordan to the east, there's not much to make you divert from the road here. To the east of Highway 90 at Beit She'an is the Jordan River crossing point between Israel and Jordan—useful for access to northern Jordan or to reach Amman from northern Israel. Taxis will take you to the border from the centre of town. You can then cross the border on foot and pick up another taxi to complete your journey on the other side.

St George's Monastery

Home to a community of monks since the fourth century, St George's Monastery is spectacularly situated on the side of Wadi Qelt, a narrow canyon on the edge of the Judean hills above Jericho. The monastery is open from 8.00 am to 12.00 noon every day, with late afternoon opening every day except Saturday. To walk through the wadi down to the monastery, take a Jerusalem taxi or come via Palestinian taxi from the Jericho end. Either way, it is an energetic 30-minute walk to the monastery. You may be able to stay the night and share a meal with the monks if there is space.

Jericho

The self-proclaimed 'oldest city in the world' overlooks the Jordan just above the Dead Sea. The vast majority of day-trippers are delivered into the marketplace and cafés around the visitor centre, whether they like it or not. With little of the city centre to walk around, this is actually not a bad option and at least you can easily explore the nearby Heights of Jericho cable car and Mount of the Temptation, on the summit of which is the Monastery of the Temptation.

Full marks go to the Palestinian authorities for their attempts to promote the city as a prime tourist destination. However, like many of the tourism initiatives in the Territories, the reality is that only a fraction of the tourists who could come here actually do so, which means that attractions like the cable car may look forlornly empty rather than buzzing with visitors.

Footsteps

The fact that most Western tourists to the region avoid the Palestinian Territories altogether will continue to be a huge source of frustration for Palestinians who are trying, often in vain, to build their own tourist and cultural infrastructure. The adage 'Build it and they will come' has been applied up and down the West Bank, without much success. The Heights of Jericho is the prime example of a multimillion-dollar investment in a very poor part of the world, which has failed to bring the benefits its backers originally hoped for.

Blame for this situation is partly down to bad PR in the West and the fact that all mass tourism operators in Israel itself actively avoid the West Bank and even tell tourists that it is not safe to travel there. Perhaps Palestinians need to work harder to promote the area, but it's not easy for them to overcome the poor perception of their country in much of the rest of the world. It does seem that many Israeli businesses attempt to put tourists off visiting the West Bank with scare stories about security. The simple truth is, they will lose money if Western tourists begin to take a more balanced trip to the region and split their time more evenly between Israel and the West Bank. There are political motivations, but, like many problems in the world, it is probably first and foremost about economics. The big Israeli tour operators have invested heavily in training multilingual guides and ordering bulletproof buses, and they need to justify their investment by skewing the reality. Anyone who says they know exactly what the situation is like in the West Bank, but has never actually been there themselves, should be treated very sceptically.

I believe that, as Christians, we have a duty to do two things while on a trip to the region: first, to honour all locations related to the journey of our Lord, be they Israeli or Palestinian, and second, to show solidarity with our many fellow Christians who are fighting for both economic and spiritual survival in the West Bank. We should never actively put ourselves or our travelling companions at risk, which does mean that we should pay attention to the news agenda, but where we can and when it is safe to do so, we should pursue every possible opportunity to engage with Christians and Christian groups. We should stay in the West Bank, hire Christian guides and use their companies and contacts, and talk with the many Christians who are working hard to ensure a future for themselves and their children in the part of the world where Jesus walked. Turning our back on that engagement and abdicating our responsibility would be a massive failure.

Although half a day is enough to do the city of Jericho and its attractions justice, you will need to hire a taxi yourself if you wish to take in St George's Monastery, which is difficult but possible to reach, either on the way out of or when returning to Jerusalem. Despite the ease of taking an organised tour, it is worth considering planning your own trip to see Jericho and the monastery. Combining all of this with a morning or afternoon at the Dead Sea in a hire car is probably the best-value option and gives you the freedom to spend more time in Jericho or at St George's if you wish to.

There are several stories in the Bible associated with Jericho. One of the best and sometimes most overlooked is that of blind Bartimaeus:

Then they came to Jericho. As Jesus and his disciples, together with a large crowd, were leaving the city, a blind man, Barti-maeus (which means 'son of Timaeus'), was sitting by the road-

side begging. When he heard that it was Jesus of Nazareth, he began to shout, 'Jesus, Son of David, have mercy on me!' Many rebuked him and told him to be quiet, but he shouted all the more, 'Son of David, have mercy on me!' Jesus stopped and said, 'Call him.' So they called to the blind man, 'Cheer up! On your feet! He's calling you.' Throwing his cloak aside, he jumped to his feet and came to Jesus. 'What do you want me to do for you?' Jesus asked him. The blind man said, 'Rabbi, I want to see.' 'Go,' said Jesus, 'your faith has healed you.' Immediately he received his sight and followed Jesus along the road.

MARK 10:46–52

You can stay in town at the Jerusalem Hotel or the Inter-continental Hotel, which both charge around £60 per night, including breakfast. As well as organised tours and car hire, you can also get to the city by taxi and bus from Ramallah, although you should allow a good couple of hours to complete the journey. This option is only really worthwhile if you are time-rich but cash-poor and intend to stay overnight in the city, perhaps going on to explore the Dead Sea region the following day. It is an enjoyable adventure to make your own way here by public transport but clearly this option is not for everyone. Hiring a car and driving down Highway 1 is a whole lot easier and not much more expensive if there are two or more of you.

Persuading your guides or tour organisers to include this part of the world may also be a challenge, but, if you wish to spend time in the West Bank while arranging your trip to Israel, insist on tailoring your itinerary to suit yourself. Groups do offer the economies of scale that should make all the options described in this chapter not just possible but also cost-effective. Do not be afraid to use your tourist muscle to get the trip you want rather than the run-of-the-mill trip that the tour operator may be keen to sell you.

Bethany

One of the most famous passages of the New Testament tells the story of Jesus' friend Lazarus, the brother of Mary and Martha in Bethany.

> *On his arrival, Jesus found that Lazarus had already been in the tomb for four days.*
> JOHN 11:17

Jesus goes on to raise Lazarus from the dead after he has been four days in the tomb and spreads fear amid his opponents. What kind of prophet can raise the dead? How powerful must Jesus really be?

> *Jesus, once more deeply moved, came to the tomb. It was a cave with a stone laid across the entrance. 'Take away the stone,' he said. 'But, Lord,' said Martha, the sister of the dead man, 'by this time there is a bad odour, for he has been there four days.' Then Jesus said, 'Did I not tell you that if you believe, you will see the glory of God?' So they took away the stone. Then Jesus looked up and said, 'Father, I thank you that you have heard me. I knew that you always hear me, but I said this for the benefit of the people standing here, that they may believe that you sent me.' When he had said this, Jesus called in a loud voice, 'Lazarus, come out!' The dead man came out, his hands and feet wrapped with strips of linen, and a cloth around his face. Jesus said to them, 'Take off the grave clothes and let him go.'*
> JOHN 11:38–44

Today, Bethany, the village of Martha, Mary and Lazarus, and also the place where Jesus spent much of his final week before entering Jerusalem, is most easily accessed via Highway 1, to the east of the city. Turn off just after the checkpoint. A hire car or organised trip are the best ways to get to the village, which contains a church dedicated to 'Saint' Lazarus. There are beautiful mosaics around the inside of the dome, including an inscription in Latin from John 11:25–26: 'He that believes in me, though he were dead, yet shall he live: and whoever lives and believes in me, shall never die.'

Beyond the church is the tomb of Lazarus, accessed down a series of steep steps. Venerated by Muslims as well as Christians, the tomb has been maintained by local Muslim families for over 400 years. Another church, dedicated to Simon the Leper, is visible behind the entrance to Lazarus' tomb.

Further reading

Paul Lawrence, *The Lion Concise Atlas of Bible History* (Lion Hudson, 2012).

Geza Vermes, *The Complete Dead Sea Scrolls in English* (Penguin, 2011).

–Chapter 6–

Nazareth and Lower Galilee

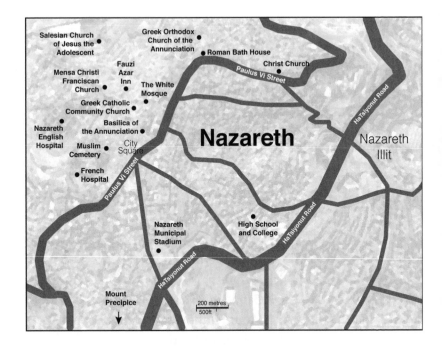

Salesian Church
of Jesus the
Adolescent

Greek Orthodox
Church of the
Annunciation

Roman Bath House

Christ Church

Paulus Vi Street

Mensa Christi
Franciscan
Church

Fauzi
Azar
Inn

The White
Mosque

HaTsiyonut Road

Greek Catholic
Community Church

Nazareth
English
Hospital

Basilica of
the Annunciation

Muslim
Cemetery

City
Square

Nazareth

Nazareth
Illit

French
Hospital

Paulus Vi Street

Nazareth
Municipal
Stadium

High School
and College

HaTsiyonut Road

HaTsiyonut Road

Mount
Precipice
↓

200 metres
500ft

Introduction

This region is a must-visit destination for Christians on
pilgrimage to the Holy Land. Of course, Jerusalem and Bethlehem draw the crowds, but if you want to walk in, see and
experience the towns where Jesus mainly lived and worked,
this is the place. It's where miracles were performed, the sick
were healed and followers gathered. Even early on, Jesus
was challenged there—for example, when he taught and was
then rejected in the local synagogue. The ancient remains of
a first-century synagogue still exists in the old town. This is
where Jesus lived as an ordinary man, then as a recognised
prophet, and finally as the Messiah. Today's Galilee is a popu-

lar destination for Israelis seeking respite from the heat of Tel Aviv and for an increasing number of international travellers keen to see another side of Israel, away from its two main cities.

It's a more laid-back region compared with the rest of Israel and an encounter with local people is much more likely to leave you feeling charmed than pressurised. Anyone who has already encountered the abruptness of a Jerusalem cabbie or shop owner will be delighted at the courtesy of a Nazareth waitress or bartender. The Galilee region is also mixed: Nazareth and the towns and villages around Lower Galilee are mostly Arab, while further north and around the lake itself, the villages and communities are mainly Jewish. In between, there are small villages in remote valleys made up of Druze and Arab-Christian communities.

Lower Galilee is also a fast-growing region close to the booming hi-tech economy of Haifa, which mixes traditional farming with a growing tourism economy. There are some excellent eco-farms, homestays and kibbutzim among the more traditional hotels and resorts.

Nazareth

This is a local success story and an example of what can happen when local people and outsiders pool their resources and ideas and visitors begin to turn around the fortunes of an almost forgotten town.

Right now, Nazareth is the up-and-coming destination within Israel. It's also a town where the local imam and rabbi work together to promote community links. Christians, Jews and Muslims work side-by-side in the Old City in a way that is not really possible to witness anywhere else, except perhaps Haifa. This collaborative approach may not have reached the city's more sectarian suburbs yet, but be in no doubt that the process has started.

Nazareth has become this shining example of interfaith and intercultural dialogue largely thanks to the vision of one man—Maoz Inon. It is Maoz's work in establishing both the Fauzi Azar Inn, with Sureida Nasser and her family, and the Jesus Trail, with David Landis and Anna Dintaman, that has put Nazareth well and truly back on the tourist map. It should have always been there, but for decades Nazareth was used by tour operators in the same way as they used Bethlehem: busloads of pilgrims stopped here just long enough to walk around the Church of the Annunciation before speeding off to spend the night elsewhere. While most visitors still fail to stay overnight, there is an increasing number who do stay. With numbers comes the economic pay-off that begins to support jobs across the whole community, and now is the time to see this process in action as the city opens new shops and restaurants on almost a weekly basis.

The town where Jesus 'grew in wisdom and stature, and in favour with God and man' (Luke 2:52) is today a large, sprawling urban centre laid out over several hillsides. Buses and car parking are found on the main road and the Church of the Annunciation is a five-minute walk up one of the adjacent steep alleyways: look for a café or a souvenir shop and the church will not be far behind. The alleyways of the old souq continue uphill from the church, with the centre of the Old City around Mary's Well, where some of the best restaurants in the region can now be found.

The Church of the Annunciation is a modern masterpiece and is the largest church in the Middle East. It is an amazing, beautiful space that deserves much wider publicity than it traditionally receives. This is arguably one of the most important Christian sites in the world and one of the world's most stunning churches. Built over Roman remains of what could have been Jesus' childhood home, the church is split into a lower crypt and a much lighter, more modern space above, with stained glass and colourful depictions of Mary, Joseph and the childhood of Jesus. As part of the same complex, slightly further uphill is the Church of St Joseph, supposed site of Joseph's carpentry shop and another important location in the early life of Jesus.

Nazareth Village, a half-mile walk south of the church and the city centre, helps to bring the past to life, with ancient farming methods on display and even a first-century lunch on the menu. It's not too kitsch and is worth a couple of hours if you are spending more than a day or two in the city.

Footsteps

It was late afternoon and the streets were dusty and still when the No. 331 Egged bus from Haifa dropped me off in the heart of Nazareth Illit, the modern Jewish suburb to the north-east of the Old City, complete with its own brand new leisure centre, shopping mall and blindingly white town hall.

But Nazareth Illit was not my ultimate destination. The Egged schedule shunned the city centre, so from here I had to walk over a mile in the heat to reach the deep valley bottom that houses the ancient heart of the city. Below me was the Church of the Annunciation, shining like a beacon alongside the minaret of the White Mosque. These landmarks guided me through narrow streets where children played and stared at me before shouting their hellos.

I passed dozens of people maintaining their cars, hosing down their drives and washing their windows. By the time I eventually found myself among the Ottoman-era mansions of the Old City, I was tired and hungry, so when I checked into the Fauzi Azar Inn and immediately struck up a conversation with two women, I happily accepted their invitation to join them for dinner.

At the Sudfeh restaurant, over entrées of haloumi and a huge bowl of salad that not even the three of us could finish, I learnt more about the area from my new companions—Belinda, a Christian tour guide originally from California, and Sue, a writer and photographer from New Zealand. We joined forces again the following morning for a free walking tour of Nazareth, expertly guided by Belinda. She explained:

> It's vital that we get more people to stay here and that local people share in the economic prosperity tourism can bring. More than two million visitors drop by Nazareth every year, but only three per cent stay overnight. That figure must change if local people are to have a stake in that tourism and see its benefits. And things are changing, thanks to Maoz. There's now even a Jewish woman—the first Jew to move back into the Old City in 20 years—because a new atmosphere of trust and cooperation has been created. There is one new business opening in the Old City every week. This was an area all but abandoned until five years ago. It's in a perfect location, halfway between Haifa and Tiberias. Great food, sites and history. It's the place where Jesus walked and played and knew his neighbours, and a place which is going through real change. What I say to people is, come and be part of it; come and contribute to what is going on here.

Belinda has been working in the Old City for more than three years now. She is a firm fixture in the local community, recognised and respected by all sides.

Another local character is Sami, of the Samira guesthouse, who has worked hard alongside Maoz and Belinda to build tourist traffic into the Old City. Sitting on the beautiful terrace of his guesthouse, Sami reflects on the positive changes that are slowly turning Nazareth from a sleepy backwater to the epicentre of a new wave of Christian pilgrimage. 'Young people from all over the world are coming to volunteer at my house, give guided tours along the Jesus Trail and teach at the orphanage,' he says.

In the evenings, the volunteers can be found sipping a drink on Sami's roof terrace and interacting with visitors. Some of them hail from the USA, Canada, Australia, Germany and Scandinavia. Many also come from Israel itself, including young IDF graduates keen to give something back to the Arab communities that they were very recently helping to police. Many will share thought-provoking stories of how they questioned orders while on duty and how they would go out of their way to engage with Arab children and elders when they could.

The sites around the city are many, but the main highlights can be covered in a day. Inside the Old City itself is the Church of the Annunciation complex, St Gabriel's Orthodox Cathedral, Mary's Well, Mary's Centre and the White Mosque. Another full day in the city will enable you to take in nearby Nazareth Village, Mount Precipice and Mount Tabor, although a hire car will be essential if you are to see all of these and get back to the city in time for dinner at one of its fantastic restaurants.

'The best falafel in town' is an accolade hard fought over, with Falafel Wissam Jabali and Falafel Abu-Hani Jabali (the two proprietors are relatives) vying for the title. Both are good and subtly different from each other, the second establishment offering more spicy accompaniments than the first. If you join the local youths and taxi drivers in the queue at either, you are bound to raise an eyebrow or two: be prepared to chat!

For a more refined dining experience, Sudfeh is superb and sits inside a beautiful old Ottoman mansion with both an open courtyard and enclosed seating areas. It serves a modern fusion of Middle Eastern and Mediterranean food. There is an atmospheric bar, upstairs meeting rooms and even an art gallery at the back of the building. Other good restaurants include Meshwar by St Mary's Well (on the corner, with big windows) and Nostalgia, which is just opposite the Post Office, just to the south of the Old City. Nostalgia goes further with the fusion theme than some of the other places in town but is amazing value for money, for the quality of food that comes out of the kitchen. Their schnitzel is rated among the best in the country.

Wherever you are staying in the Old City, it means visiting the Fauzi Azar Inn at least once. Just north of the souq, the Fauzi is now a local (and, increasingly, national and international) institution. It is a centre of information and activity even if you don't actually stay here. More guesthouses have opened up around it as visitor numbers have steadily increased, the best being the Samira guesthouse along the alley on Sibat Kawar. The original vision of Maoz Inon at the Fauzi Azar has shaped the entire tourism industry in the city. It's not just about casual tourists, however. The number of Christian pilgrims who are beginning to realise they can stay here and walk (at least some of) the Jesus Trail rather than just pass through on a bus tour is making Nazareth a great alternative to Tiberias as a base for exploring the wider region.

In the words of Maoz Inon:

Dialogue is the first step towards agreement. Without actually sitting down with one another and talking, there will never be progress. But we never meant to start something big here; we only wanted to do our bit for promoting tourism and bringing people into Nazareth and the Galilee. It was never meant to be this big peace initiative. We just wanted to bring people in and build some economic activity which could be shared by everyone. I'm not political. But if you build bridges, then it invariably brings the different sides together. It's a side-effect of working together. It takes time, of course, but no one's in any rush because we all want something sustainable as well as practical and to build something that is of benefit to the whole community.

The fact that Maoz and his friends are building something from the ground up has not been lost on the wider world. Recipient of a Virgin Holidays travel award and a partner in further tourism-based ventures in Jerusalem, Maoz sees a bright future for Israel, as long as its people work together:

Some people thought I was mad for partnering with Arabs and promoting tourism throughout the whole country, but fundamentally this is about giving visitors what they want and need and allowing everyone to share in that. And what visitors have always told me is that they want a more authentic experience, away from the one-week tours with a security detail. What kind of message do those kind of experiences give people visiting Israel for the first time?

Maoz is obviously not the only one. Israel is full of young entrepreneurs, keen on sharing this vision. Maoz again:

We have the opportunity to rise above our differences and build something here which will deliver an economic benefit for everyone. Sometimes it takes an outsider to see a solution, someone who can step away from the cultural or religious context and just see people for what they are. There are many Westerners of all kinds of backgrounds working hard in Israel to bring the country together. I want a Muslim from Indonesia or a Jew from New York or a Christian from England all to find the same joy and positivity within Israel when they come here. And I want them to go home to their own communities and talk about how great Israel is to visit, and come back again and again.

Budget accommodation in Nazareth includes the excellent Fauzi Azar Inn, with its choice of comfortable dorms or atmospheric private rooms, and the smaller but equally cosy and friendly Samira guesthouse, which is also in the middle of the Old City. Standard choices are few, but there are good reviews of the Casa Maria Hotel on the main road into town. For the luxury option, the only hotel worth the money is the Golden Crown Hotel, on the way out to Mount Precipice. It is a little tired, but it has good facilities, such as a pool and gym, as well as views of Mount Tabor. You will need to take a taxi to get into the centre of town from here, and the food can reportedly be a little hit or miss.

Cana

On the third day a wedding took place at Cana in Galilee. Jesus' mother was there, and Jesus and his disciples had also been invited.

JOHN 2:1–2

Sounds simple enough, doesn't it? The site of Jesus' first miracle is an unassuming place, a small Arab town on the road to Nazareth, very much off the beaten track, but that also makes it typical of this part of Israel. Villages and towns can be found tucked away behind hills and forests, away from main roads. At the same time, Cana is only a matter of minutes from Nazareth and is on the bus route north of the city, towards Highway 77.

Located up an alley behind the main street is the Church of the Wedding Feast—a bright white Franciscan property with a habit of turning away from services those who are not part of a booked group. However, the church is a cheery and attractive space with a high dome, so it's well worth persevering to get into it. Its altar sits over the site where Jesus reportedly turned water into wine for the benefit of his friends and family; in the basement you'll find an example of the 30-litre stone jars involved. Next door is an even less accessible Orthodox church (look for the colourful flags in the garden), but try to find the guardian, who will at least tell you when the church is open.

The cafés of the town centre give you a taste of modern life for Israeli Arabs, with plenty of pitta bread and hummus stands, falafel stalls and sheesha smoking pipes for sale among the postcards and ice creams. There is also plenty of fresh fruit and veg around, should you be tempted to make your own dinner.

The town is the endpoint of the first day of the Jesus Trail. If you would like to spend the night there, try the Wedding Feast guesthouse, immediately behind the churches (follow the narrow alleyway to the side of the Church of the Wedding Feast), which has double rooms from around £40 per person per night (including evening meal, bed and breakfast) and excellent views.

Mount Tabor

Since the fourth century, Mount Tabor has been claimed as the scene of the transfiguration, where Jesus revealed his true nature to disciples John, Peter and James. While most biblical scholars cite Mount Hermon (see pages 177–78) as the location for this event, it is to Mount Tabor that most pilgrims will travel, and it's easy to see why: affording sweeping views of the Jezreel valley from the summit of this dramatic peak is the beautiful Church of the Transfiguration.

About eight days after Jesus said this, he took Peter, John and James with him and went up onto a mountain to pray. As he was praying, the appearance of his face changed, and his clothes became as bright as a flash of lightning. Two men, Moses and Elijah, appeared in glorious splendour, talking with Jesus. They spoke about his departure, which he was about to bring to fulfilment at Jerusalem. Peter and his companions were very sleepy, but when they became fully awake, they saw his glory and the two men standing with him. As the men were leaving Jesus, Peter said to him, 'Master, it is good for us to be here. Let us put up three shelters—one for you, one for Moses and one for Elijah.' (He did not know what he was saying.)

While he was speaking, a cloud appeared and covered them, and they were afraid as they entered the cloud. A voice came from the cloud, saying, 'This is my Son, whom I have chosen; listen to him.' When the voice had spoken, they found that Jesus was alone. The disciples kept this to themselves and did not tell anyone at that time what they had seen.

LUKE 9:28–36

Mount Tabor is an easy side-trip from Nazareth or Tiberias, especially if you have a car. It's also possible (although not easy) to get there by bus via the village of Dabburiyah and, of course, by taxi. Haggle hard if going for the latter option, however, and try to hire a driver for half a day so that he can wait for you at the top and ensure you don't get stuck. Having said that, there are usually plenty of minibuses plying the road up and down the mountain, and those who feel fit enough can hike up in about an hour and a half.

Yet another Antonio Barluzzi-designed church, the site on the very summit of the mountain is one of the most beautiful spots in Israel. The church itself makes the most of the light that floods in and has two beautiful side chapels, one dedicated to Moses and the other to Elijah. Uniquely, the nave sits at a middle level, with two tiers cascading down from it. The altar and windows in the crypt make a dazzling display with the equally stunning frescoes set against the white stone of the walls.

Footsteps

The work of Italian architect Antonio Barluzzi adorns Israel, and his legacy is his beautiful churches, which pay homage to their setting and encourage light and brightness to flood into wide-open internal spaces. The Church of the Transfiguration is considered by many as his masterpiece: the interior of the church has a 'wow' factor that few others in the region can match.

Barluzzi was a Franciscan monk who spent most of the interwar period in Palestine, building on behalf of the Catholic Church, who were the overseers of Christian churches in the Holy Land. As well as his church on Mount Tabor, he designed the Church of All Nations at Gethsemane, Dominus Flevit on the Mount of Olives, the Church of the Beatitudes by the Sea of Galilee and the Church of the Angels at the Shepherds' Fields near Bethlehem.

Today these churches contribute to many of the Christian pilgrimage sites across the Holy Land. On a typical visit, pilgrims may come across seven or eight of Barluzzi's churches, often without realising that they are all by the same architect and all built in the interwar period. A plaque on the east wall of the Church of the Transfiguration, next to the main entrance, commemorates this important figure in the history of the Christian church in the Holy Land.

The Jesus Trail

Connecting the lower and upper Galilee and Jesus' home town to the site of his ministry, the Jesus Trail has quickly taken off as a 'must' for both independent travellers and groups wishing to connect more authentically with everyday life 2000 years ago. At the same time, the trail's founders are very much concerned with placing Jesus in the modern world and encouraging pilgrims to encounter the many faces of Jesus in the people of the Galilee today.

We know that Jesus often made his way around the region, courtesy of the grace and generosity of others. Whether he was provided with a room for the night, a meal, companionship or a donkey on which to ride, we know from the Gospels that Jesus could not have conducted any of his ministry without help and patronage. Today we can emulate that humility and place ourselves in the hands of new friends along a trail that stretches right across the Galilee, taking in towns and villages of every persuasion. The trail is another way in which we can follow Jesus' lead and copy him. If you want to get closer to the historical Jesus, there's no better way than to walk the paths he would have walked, stay in the towns he once knew, and be a pilgrim in the locations of his ministry.

None of this is new, of course—Christian pilgrims have been coming here for centuries—but there was little before in terms of joined-up tourism provision, bringing together all the different elements of the Galilee. The Israel National Trail cuts across the route now established so successfully by the team of Maoz Inon, David Landis and Anna Dintaman. Between them, they have worked tirelessly with the Israeli National Park and Nature Authority and local businesspeople to make the Jesus Trail a reality not just for pilgrims but also for locals. This helps to make the trail unique. The partnerships built up along the way also bring Christian values to bear on modern-day reality.

And what a reality it is! Where once there was little or no infrastructure to support a pilgrimage to this part of the country, there is now a network of paths linked to hotels, kibbutzim and places to stay and eat all along the route. But the focus remains firmly on following the pathways of the historical Jesus and his disciples as they travelled this area. While the built environment may be new, it is thrilling to have the opportunity to walk through the hills, woods and fields that have been around since his time, knowing that his feet probably trod these same routes.

As Anna Dintaman reflects in the excellent *Hiking the Jesus Trail* guidebook, 'Walking is a humble, non-threatening way to encounter new people, bring to life historical and spiritual texts and, through the physical challenge and removal from ordinary life, also grow to know ourselves better.' These ambitions may appear lofty when read in isolation but when Anna's words are lived out on the ground in the towns and villages of the Galilee, they make perfect sense.

The trek detailed here follows the classic four-day itinerary of Nazareth–Cana, Cana–Lavi, Lavi–Arbel and finally Arbel–Capernaum. The trail could be covered in three days, however, with either Cana–Arbel or Lavi–Capernaum taken as alternative single, long days of around 25 kilometres. The trail often covers rough ground, which can be replaced by less interesting but faster road walking. Whichever route is picked, it can always be improvised. Accommodation should ideally be booked in advance, although many of the lodgings are sizable or flexible enough to cope with walk-in customers.

Day One sees you climb a total of 406 steps out of Nazareth's Old City, starting at the Church of the Annunciation, before gaining the hill above Nazareth from which it's possible to catch a stunning vista that has inspired generations of local people. From the Mediterranean and the curve of Haifa Bay in the west to the Sea of Galilee in the east and snow-capped Mount Hermon in the north, the view encompasses almost the entire route from its source to final destination. It's very exciting to be able to see exactly what terrain awaits you on the trail over the next few days.

Coming down into the valley to the north of Nazareth, the Jesus Trail makes a beeline for one of the area's most popular archaeological sites—Zippori. This national park contains remains of the Galilee region's former Roman and Jewish capital, spread out over 200 acres. Starting with the ancient aqueduct and water system and finishing at the Jewish town and synagogue, the site is impressive and, again, affords excellent views across to Mount Hermon, Zefat and the hills leading down to the shores of the Sea of Galilee in the distance.

Zippori National Park is open every day, including the sabbath, with a 50 NIS entry fee. There are good toilet and refreshment facilities, making this a natural place to break for lunch. As Gili, one of the volunteers from the Fauzi Azar Inn and a guide on the trail, explains:

Sometimes the weather impacts a hike: it's often raining in winter and almost too hot to hike in the summer. But on a clear spring day you can see all the way to Haifa and the Med from the ridge above Nazareth and the Galilee in the distance. A walk around Zippori is my favourite leg of the trail. It's well worth an extended detour to take in the ancient tunnels and see the plants and animals which have made the park their home.

Ten kilometres east from Zippori, through ancient pine forest and high on a ridge above the valley, the path eventually brings you to the Arab village of Mashhad. From here it's just a short walk downhill to Cana, where guesthouse options might enable you to spend the night. If fully booked, it is also easy to catch a bus back to Nazareth, and taxis between each stage of the trail are another option.

Day Two sees you regain the ridge above Cana and trek east through woodland, before dropping down in front of an army base and coming out at Golani Junction, where two major highways intersect. Lavi Forest begins here, and a subway beneath the main road will bring you just to the east of the small Golani Brigade Museum, next door to a McDonalds.

A stay at Kibbutz Lavi is a welcome dose of luxury at the end of the second day's hike. A charming and peaceful place, the hotel is now one of the foremost four-star resorts in the region. Originally founded in the 1950s by British Jews returning to the area, the fundamental principles of socialist community living are still alive and well here. Each member of the kibbutz performs the job best suited to them and receives the amount of support, accommodation and holiday that they need in return. Some people have remained in the kibbutz all their lives. Some young people come for a few years, begin to raise their children here and then leave. But the magic of the life is not lost on visitors, and staying over *Shabbat*, when a seven-course meal is served and groups of Israelis sing together well into the evening, makes a lasting impression.

The kibbutz is, of course, also a great place for an extended stay, with its beautiful hillside gardens, excellent pool, and walking and running track marked out around the hilltop. It's a joyous, peaceful haven away from the highway and perfectly placed halfway along the Jesus Trail. Quoting Maoz or the Jesus Trail will also secure preferential rates at the hotel and ensure that you are perfectly looked after. Hospitality is in people's blood here and the chairman of the kibbutz runs a free two-hour guided walk every Sunday—even if you're the only person to turn up.

Day Three provides an interesting trek over one of Israel's most important Crusader sites—the Horns of Hattin, twin peaks with magnificent views—down to Nebi Shu'eib, the home of the Druze community, and eventually to the head of the Arbel Valley. An hour or two in the valley will bring you up against ever-steepening hill sides, but you can cut back up to the southern side of the valley before the cliffs start. Arbel village is a fine place for relaxation and an evening among other tourists and locals at the end of the third day. There are some high-quality, welcoming guesthouses, like

Arbel Holiday Village, which has Scandinavian-style cabins and peaceful terraces on which to sit out the evening. This guesthouse also has a pool and games room for those who wish to stay active, and good food from hosts Beni and Sylvia.

Day Four is long and challenging but the hardest section— up and over the Arbel cliffs—can be avoided if you would rather retrace your steps to the bottom of the Arbel Valley and head straight for the village of Wadi Hamam at the foot of the Arbel. For those fit enough to descend the cliffs themselves, there is a steep path that skirts the rocks (a few handholds are necessary) before taking a line beneath the steepest part of the cliff-face until it reaches the ruins inside the caves. By early afternoon and for the rest of the day, the cliffs provide some merciful shade, and this is another excellent place to sit, reflect and perhaps enjoy some lunch or a Bible reading with the Sea of Galilee before you and the valleys leading back to Nazareth behind you. There are always excellent views of the entire Galilee region and rising heights of the Golan behind, especially at twilight and dawn, when the landscape takes on brilliant hues of purple, pink and gold. Clambering over and through the ruined caves will also bring home the story of this site—how Hasmonean rebels resisted Roman attack for several months during the Jewish wars. The siege ended only when the Romans lowered themselves from the cliffs above in baskets and threw burning tar into the caves.

The final stretch of the trail runs along the water's edge at the Sea of Galilee and ends at Capernaum, home of Jesus' ministry. By then you will have had three, four or even more days to forget about some of the demands of home, encounter other people, share stories and be refreshed along the way. As Anna Dintaman again so eloquently puts it, 'We invite you to fearlessly step into this challenge, following the example of Jesus. Trust in God and the image of God reflected in the people you meet. Be blessed and be a blessing.'

Footsteps

It was unbelievably hot on the trail. My friend Felix and I had risen at 7.00 am and begun trekking from Kibbutz Lavi in what felt like midday heat, hours before the actual middle of the day. By the time we had climbed the Horns of Hattin, the temperature was hitting the mid 30s Celsius. We'd drunk about half of our entire day's supply of water but only walked about a fifth of the distance.

It was going to be a long day.

After the volcanic and historical sites of Hattin, we descended to the Druze shrine at Nebi Shu'eib, which gently enticed us with flags and golden domes. The sight of the religion's wondrously ornate headquarters, perched dramatically beneath the white cliffs, felt like a draw too good to miss. But it wasn't to be good timing: it was a 'female visitors only' day, the guard at the entrance gate explained, and, despite our pleading, we had to walk away disappointed. At least the guard allowed us to fill our water bottles!

An hour later we were amid the ruins of the mosque at the long-abandoned village of Hittin, and it was far too temptingly peaceful to do anything but stop and rest. We sat in the shade of the mid-afternoon and read passages from the Bible as we ate our rations. The heat continued to build and rise from the ground around us, as if we were sitting on the edge of a volcano. An hour turned easily into two as we polished off our food and almost all the rest of our water, reading and relaxing in the shade. A walk around the dusty ruins of Hittin soon brought us back into contact with the energy-sapping, skin-burning rays of the summertime sun.

Hittin was a prosperous Arab village until 1948, but, as in nearly 500 other Arab towns and villages located in what became Israel, Hittin's population found it preferable to leave than remain in a valley that had witnessed fighting and bloodshed. Many of Hittin's inhabitants fled to neighbouring Jordan and its Palestinian-majority West Bank, or on into Lebanon or Syria, but some remained close by and settled in larger Arab towns such as Cana, Tur'an and Nazareth. The ruined village now acts as a stark reminder of the issue of Palestinian return: it is all about the right of Palestinians to return to the towns and villages they once called home. Successive Israeli governments have fiercely resisted discussing it, or have only included it in wider peace offers, despite the demands of almost one million Palestinians who wish to return to the towns and villages of their ancestors.

The reason why there are so many Palestinian refugee camps within Palestine (55 camps in total, housing more than a million people) isn't because people can't settle in the West Bank or Gaza, but because they thought their removal from Israel in 1948 or 1967 would only be temporary: they are still waiting to go home. Will former Arab villages inside Israel one day rise from the ashes, in the same way that Jewish towns and cities have done? For successive Israeli governments, the issue has always been tied up with their own concepts of land and population. To add another million Arabs to the Israeli population would risk long-term Jewish hegemony. Right now, with the lack of any constructive talks between the Israeli and Palestinian sides over the issue, the answer seems as elusive as it has always been.

When we finally left the ruins of Hittin behind, I did it with my hood firmly up around my head to try to deflect the worst of the sun. Despite the temperature and the black colour of my hoody, the top did protect me from potentially horrendous sunburn. The walk down into the Arbel Valley again brought home the reality that these paths are the same as those walked by our Lord and his disciples.

Occasionally paved with brilliant-white cobbles, but usually just stones and grass, the route followed the stream through the very middle of the valley, with its clusters of goats and cows munching in the shade of the olive trees. Felix and I reminisced on our homes and on previous journeys we'd taken. We discussed our faith, how we both tried to follow the vivid example of Jesus' life, and how much closer we felt to him right then. I wondered whether Jesus had ever had the same kinds of discussions, as he'd walked these roughly hewn paths with his friends.

We took to heart how tough the environment was, even though modern villages and amenities were only ever a few kilometres away. We both asked out loud how Jesus coped without sunscreen or fizzy drinks or easily packaged food. Were there more people walking these trails then, and, if so, were there regular stopping points where hikers from village to village could catch up on refreshments and provisions before hitting the trail again? We knew that Roman roads of the time were very well designed and there were taverns and inns every 20 miles or so, to enable the marching legions to rest for the night. These inns were also available for the travelling salesmen of the day, commercial travellers, or those off to see family in a different part of the country. With food on the menu and stabling for horses, the inns were the precursor of today's hotels. The food may have changed, and stables may have been replaced by car parks, but the principle is the same.

What the Romans had learnt had been forgotten a thousand years later, when the bungling Crusaders, walking the same route, reached the Tur'an valley but chose not to camp overnight next to a good water source. Instead they marched on for Tiberias, only to find the Mamluk army ready and waiting for them at the Horns of Hattin. All water and food supplies were now closed to the Crusader army—and they paid the price, being defeated and driven from the Holy Land for ever.

Paul's conversion on the road to Damascus could also have taken place at a point such as this, in the middle of a rural valley in the middle of a roasting-hot day. The Roman road that skirts Lavi would almost certainly have continued down into the Arbel Valley at some point before crossing the plains to the west of the Sea of Galilee on its way to Capernaum. Eventually it would have continued the short distance over the mountains into Syria. We can't say at which exact point Paul may have experienced his conversion, but it may well have been somewhere just like this.

About noon, as I came near Damascus, suddenly a bright light from heaven flashed around me. I fell to the ground and heard a voice say to me, 'Saul! Saul! Why do you persecute me?'
Acts 22:6–7

It may have been a mirage, a hallucination, a dream or a direct message from another place, but Paul responded the only way he knew how: he went from being Saul, chief persecutor of the Christians, to Paul, the apostle of Christ. Never in the history of the world was someone transformed more completely than he was at that moment.

Israel in summer is a blisteringly hot and unforgiving place, and hiking (or any other form of exercise, for that matter) should not be undertaken lightly. The obvious key consideration is to remain hydrated at all times, and carrying enough water in a rucksack may put you off even beginning a walk, since the weight of the water could be an issue.

The key is to minimise all other luggage, since water and a small number of snacks have to come first. A good solution may be to leave your main bag at a previous lodging place. Hostels are the most relaxed places for this arrangement, and will charge the lowest prices. Another way is to send your main bag ahead by taxi to your next accommodation stop, ensuring that your belongings are ready and waiting for you at the end of the day's hike.

If you stay overnight in Arbel village, the final day's hike is definitely the most dramatic. After walking along the edge of the 400-metre high cliffs of Mount Arbel and marvelling at the view across the sea, you will find that the path drops steeply back into the Arbel Valley before the historic cliffs. Later, corner shops and the nearby garage are just a short walk on from Wadi Hamam (a bedouin Muslim village of more than 1000 people) and can keep you refreshed until you head out for the final ten kilometres leading to Tabgha and the Mount of Beatitudes.

This is a flat and straightforward stretch of walk—or it would be on a mild day. In the heat of summer it is an arduous and taxing journey, which will again remind you of what it must have been like 2000 years ago. Completing any substantial trek in sandals or other open footwear, along these kinds of paths, would have been a major undertaking. Not only would it have been necessary to plan the stopping-places along the trail, but you would also have had to think about where to buy new clothes or footwear if existing possessions wore out. Today's traveller has the mall and the superstore to make life easier, but what if those conveniences weren't available? How would we cope with the harsh conditions of a hike like this with no modern infrastructure around us?

If the path does become too taxing, it's always possible to find a route directly east, between the banana plantations, back to the main Highway 90, which runs from Tiberias towards Upper Galilee. The final two kilometres of the Jesus Trail follow this main road, involving an inevitable climb and subsequent descent to Tabgha—home of the Church of the Loaves and Fishes (or Church of the Multiplication: see information on page 171). This small but pretty church on the shores of the Sea of Galilee is a good place to stop on a hot day: clean toilets, a well-stocked shop and café and the quiet shaded precincts of the church itself await weary travellers. The Franciscans are welcoming hosts and this is yet another example of a place to pause, rest and reflect upon your way.

And he told the people to sit down on the grass. Taking the five loaves and the two fish and looking up to heaven, he gave thanks and broke the loaves. Then he gave them to the disciples, and the disciples gave them to the people. They all ate and were satisfied, and the disciples picked up twelve basketfuls of broken pieces that were left over. The number of those who ate was about five thousand men, besides women and children.

Matthew 14:19–21

The simple yet beautiful interior of the church includes the remains of a sixth-century mosaic in the floor, which once belonged to a much older church on the site. The loaves and fishes motif can still be made out today and reinforces one of the most talked-about and radically subversive acts of Jesus' ministry. To provide food, and plenty of it, to a crowd of ordinary people who may have travelled, like today's hiker, several hours or even days to reach the lake was tantamount to treason. It not only highlighted the inability of the occupying Roman forces to feed everyone properly, but it also showed that the same people would make personal sacrifices—even going thirsty and hungry—in order to realise the chance of watching and hearing Jesus speak. Not only that, but these listeners were then miraculously rewarded for their loyalty and witness. Who had ever heard of such things? This preacher's ability to draw a crowd was unprecedented. John the Baptist had held the mantle before, but Jesus was taking it several steps beyond. He could not only match John's popular appeal but could also look after those who came to follow him—as if his promises and predictions were real, as if they contained an inherent and self-evident truth.

Jesus was going to be a very challenging character for the Roman and Jewish authorities to deal with.

Further reading

Jacob Firsel, *Go to Galilee: A travel guide for Christian pilgrims* (Village to Village Press, 2011).

Anna Dintaman and David Landis, *Hiking the Jesus Trail* (2nd edn) (Village to Village Press, 2013).

Geza Vermes, *Christian Beginnings: From Nazareth to Nicaea, AD30–325* (Penguin, 2013).

–Chapter 7–

Upper Galilee and the Golan Heights

This is the region where Jesus conducted so much of his ministry. Along with the adjacent Golan Heights, it is a beautiful, accessible and affordable part of the Holy Land, which richly rewards an extended stay.

❖ Introduction
❖ Tiberias
❖ The Sea of Galilee
❖ River Jordan
❖ Tabgha
❖ Capernaum
❖ The Church of the Beatitudes
❖ Zefat
❖ Tel Dan and Banias
❖ Nimrod Castle
❖ Mount Hermon and the Golan Heights

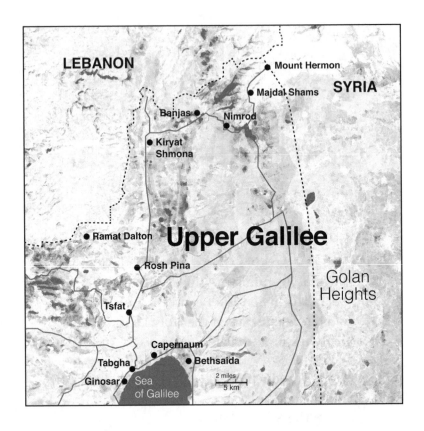

Introduction

Throughout all four Gospels the Galilee region looms large, and for obvious reasons. Once Jesus departs his home town of Nazareth, he moves to nearby Capernaum on the shores of the Middle East's largest lake. Barely 40 miles separate the two towns, but they were, and remain, very different places. Nazareth was a small provincial village in the hills, Capernaum a large trading centre close to a major Roman road connecting the Mediterranean and the city of Damascus.

Today the roles are reversed: Capernaum is in ruins and Nazareth is a bustling, mixed city of almost 60,000, with historic sites and welcoming people—Israeli Arabs and Jews alike—eager to show you their town.

Galilee, though, still captures the feeling of the Gospels in a way that no other location can. Two thousand years ago, Jesus kept on returning to Galilee: his home and heart remained in the region. He visited Jerusalem, and 'returned to Galilee'. He went out to the desert, and 'returned to Galilee.' He visited the coast at Tyre and Sidon, and 'returned to Galilee'.

As Jesus' ministry took off and people got to know that there was a travelling prophet living in their midst, he purposely made his base in a place where his ideas would gain traction and become more widespread. He found friends and favour in Capernaum, described in Matthew 9:1 as 'his own town'. In Galilee he was always welcome until he began to face politically motivated opposition in the months leading up to his death: 'News about him spread through the whole countryside. He was teaching in their synagogues, and everyone praised him' (Luke 4:14–15).

Capernaum was undoubtedly a place where Jesus found favour at first, but during the final year of his life he also had to face the kind of rejection that forewarned him and his disciples of what would come when he made his final journey to Jerusalem. Perhaps, as the challenge of Jesus' ministry sank in and people recognised the implications of his message, they turned against this new teacher about whom they had previously been so enthusiastic. One of the obvious questions, then, is why? What changed, and when? A clue lies within the landscape of Galilee itself. It has always been a fertile region, strategically important for anyone who cares about trade with both the east and the west. The Romans could not run the risk of ignoring it; equally, the Jewish authorities could not control it in the way they could control Jerusalem. The Galilee was not quite the provincial backwater it's sometimes portrayed as having been in New Testament times.

As we have seen, this was one of the most vital trade routes in the Roman empire, connecting Damascus and kingdoms further east with the Mediterranean and the very heart of the empire to the west. Anyone unsettling the population here could very quickly spread dissent to the rest of the region and beyond. Even before he left the Galilee, Jesus was in danger. His words as a radical preacher were as dangerous as anything the authorities could imagine. The last Messiah-like figure who had travelled the region, inadvertently fomenting dissent—John the Baptist—had paid for his words with his life. There was no way Jesus and his followers were going to be left alone.

The Galilee was a centre of Jewish learning and culture, an alternative to Jerusalem for those who wanted to build upon traditional Judaism and reshape it for different times. The Kabbalah movement was founded in the mystical hilltop town of Zefat, for example, and the kibbutz movement of the 19th and 20th centuries was also founded in the region. (For a detailed explanation of the Kabbalah movement—a mystical Jewish tradition based on esoteric teachings—visit www.kabbalah.com.) Today, the relative quiet of the Galilee can come as a very welcome contrast to the hustle and bustle and dust and heat of Jerusalem or Tel Aviv. Less than three hours north but a world away geographically, the fertile agricultural land around the lake presents a gentler, greener version of the Holy Land than the drier landscape further south. From Tel Aviv, the Galilee region is a two-hour drive on good motorway-standard roads for most of the way; add another half an hour from Jerusalem. Egged has regular buses from Tel Aviv, Jerusalem and Haifa into the largest city, Tiberias. They run several times a day, with prices starting at around £10, one way.

Getting around the Galilee yourself is best done in a hire car: a local firm, Eldan, hires out economy cars from less than £20 per day if booked in advance online (see www.eldan. co.il/en). It is feasible to hitchhike or take local buses but they are infrequent and, although distances are not great, it can take hours to reach the Golan Heights by bus.

Most of the sites relating to the Gospels are either free to enter or charge only a small fee, such as the 3 NIS for Capernaum. Israeli National Parks charge between 22 and 29 NIS per person per site, but a group ticket will bring considerable savings. With a car, the wider region is easily within reach, including locations such as Caesarea Philippi (also known as Banias) and Mount Hermon. This mountain was once fully within Syria and rises to 2814 metres, offering skiing in the winter and hiking in the summer. It's a shame that the region lacks the tourists who flock further south, since it is both cooler and more beautiful than many other parts of the country and will amply reward a stay of several days.

A bicycle is the other perfect way to get around: cycling around the lake should present no problem for any reasonably fit cyclist, as long as it's not done in midsummer. The roads are quiet and a round route of about 30 miles will take in all of the main locations around the Sea of Galilee and get you back to Tiberias well before sunset. A longer, multi-day trip would be to cycle along the quiet northern roads up to Mount Hermon and back. Note that the roads can be very hilly and it is vital to carry plenty of water with you if you're on a bike. There are few shops and villages to the north and east of the Sea of Galilee, so always take at least one spare inner tube and tyre levers as well as refreshments. Don't cycle through the middle of the day in summer, otherwise you run a real risk of heatstroke.

The same rule applies to hikers. More and more people are choosing to walk through the region, and this is another way of slowing down your travel and getting you more closely in touch with both the landscape and the people along the way. Not only is it a more authentic way of travel, but it is more in keeping with the style of travel undertaken by Jesus and his disciples. The Jesus Trail website (www.jesustrail.com) and the accompanying guidebook contain tons of information not just on the paths that make up the trail but also on local accommodation, eating and transportation choices between Nazareth and Capernaum. If you fancy a bit of luxury, that can be accommodated too: there is a wide selection of value-for-money resort-style hotels in Tiberias, including some along the shore of the Sea of Galilee averaging around £60 per night for a twin bedroom and breakfast. Among them are the Arcadia and the trio of Leonardo resorts: the Leonardo Club is the pick of these.

An excellent alternative option is to stay outside the town and experience kibbutz life at places such as Kibbutz Lavi, where luxurious rooms, a 20-metre swimming pool, rose gardens and excellent food can be had for around £60 per night per person on a half-board basis. Kibbutzim are a popular way to stay in the region and there are many spread out around the lake. One of the biggest and best is Kibbutz Nof Ginosar, close to Tabgha, which is also home to a first-century fishing boat, rescued from the lake in 1986. Lovingly restored, is serves as a reminder of the kind of boat that was used here for fishing at the time of Jesus.

The kibbutz—a socialist collective farming movement—has risen and fallen in popularity. In the 1960s and 1970s it was a favourite option for gap-year students from around the world, and Israel's kibbutzim still attract people looking for some time out from the traditional demands of their own society. Their accommodation options are often of a high standard and spending a night here makes a change from staying in hostels and hotels.

Unlike in Jerusalem, specifically Christian accommodation in the Galilee is thin on the ground, but many of the guest-houses in the Arab towns are owned and run by Christians. They give you the opportunity to interact with locals and see something of their way of life, while eating and drinking with families and talking, always, about Israeli–Arab relations.

If you are hiking or cycling, it is worth repeating, once again, that heatstroke is a very real and constant danger. Hiking in the summer in Israel is considered almost impossible, due to the inability to access enough water en route. Spring and autumn offer much better options for hiking but will still require you to drink around four litres of water every day. Don't ever think this doesn't apply to you: many people die from heatstroke while hiking in Israel every year, including locals.

Tiberias

An Israeli seaside town has been built around the site of the Roman ruins of Tiberias. It's not an especially pretty place but its location, on a steep hillside leading down to the lake, is very impressive and makes up for the lack of charm in its buildings. It has all the shops and restaurants you could need, especially on the waterfront below the Leonardo hotels or at the brand new mall that has opened further into the town, next to the bus station. There is also a very big out-of-town complex just off the main Highway 77, at Poriya Junction, with a large supermarket, fashion and electrical stores, coffee shops and restaurants.

The appeal of the town has much to do with the tiny market stalls and restaurants that throng the avenues down to the lakeshore. The beauty of Tiberias lies in its setting on the steep slopes overlooking the lake and in its convenience and excellent transport links. Although alternative regional bases have much more character, the city is a convenient place for a stay in the Galilee and is significantly cheaper than either Tel Aviv or Jerusalem. From the city, nowhere is far away and, with a day or two's car hire, you can get around all of the biblical sites, plus much of the Golan Heights, before heading back south or perhaps moving over to the coast. With several days and overnight stays in places like Zefat, the Golan will really come to life in your mind and give you a glimpse of an alternative lifestyle seldom seen in other parts of Israel. It's not quite bucolic, but certainly more in tune with the natural setting than the cities or coastal strip.

The Tiberias bus station is slightly uphill, behind the main shopping streets, and has regular services to the region and further afield, with up to a dozen buses a day to Tel Aviv and Jerusalem (from 20 NIS, one way). Haifa is served hourly for around 15 NIS. Budget accommodation includes the Aviv Hotel and Hostel in the centre of town, while the best in the standard bracket is the Astoria (although it is almost a mile uphill). The Scots Hotel on the waterfront is the best of the luxury-priced accommodation, with superb food and rooms.

Eating out is easy if you are looking for fast food, but choose carefully from the seafront restaurants: the ones slightly inland are better value than those offering sea views.

The Sea of Galilee

Boat trips regularly ply the waters of the lake from Tiberias, typically calling at Capernaum and Ein Gedi. On the far shore of the lake is Bethsaida, where Jesus may have fed the 5000 (see also information about the site at Tabgha, on page 171). Despite the steep entrance fee (60 NIS with a car), it's a peaceful spot on the banks of the Jordan and is perfect for a picnic in the shade—just as it was 2000 years ago.

As previously discussed, there are a variety of ways to travel around the lake. A hire car is the easiest and cheapest option and will give you the freedom to explore further into the Golan Heights. For those who wish to experience the region on horseback, the ranch at Vered HaGalil is the best-known riding school and hire centre in the area. A day-long trek will cost around £40 and the centre also has guest rooms and cottages, again priced at around £40 per night, as well as a café and a shop. All in all, it's a very peaceful way to see the Galilee and experience the serenity of the area (visit www.veredhagalil.com).

When the apostles returned, they reported to Jesus what they had done. Then he took them with him and they withdrew by themselves to a town called Bethsaida, but the crowds learned about it and followed him. He welcomed them and spoke to them about the kingdom of God, and healed those who needed healing. Late in the afternoon the Twelve came to him and said, 'Send the crowd away so they can go to the surrounding villages

and countryside and find food and lodging, because we are in a
remote place here.' He replied, 'You give them something to eat.'
Luke 9:10–13

River Jordan

At Bethsaida, the River Jordan—a mixture of snow melt from
distant Mount Hermon and Galilee's relatively high rainfall—
flows into the northern end of the lake. Further north, near
to Rosh Pina, are a number of rafting centres offering half-
day trips down the river from 150 NIS per person, but at
Bethsaida the river can be something of an anticlimax. It's
so shallow that you could almost wade across it, which, of
course, made it an easy and popular place for ritual bathing
and baptism.

Today there is a popular baptism site at Yardenit, just off
the main road running south of Tiberias towards Beit She'an.
Though not peaceful, it is an easy spot to dunk your toes or
even your whole self in the river, just as many thousands do
every week. The visitor centre charges 40 NIS to hire robes
and towels but you can ignore this if you wish, walk down to
the water and suit yourself.

The Jordan both enters and leaves the Sea of Galilee, and
the river's source is to the north of the lake, in the Golan.
One of the best springs rises at the Tel Dan nature reserve
(29 NIS entry fee), where you can watch the water gushing
beneath you as you stand on a wooden bridge. (A game of
Pooh Sticks would be over very quickly!)

Down at Beit She'an (a crossroads town on the main
highway south to Jerusalem, as well as on the east–west road
into Jordan) there is a superb national park built around the
site of the best Roman ruins in Israel. As well as colonnaded

streets and a huge amphitheatre, there is a forum and hill from which the whole site can be seen. The national park is open every day from 8.00 am to 5.30 pm, 25 NIS entry fee.

Tabgha

The Church of the Multiplication is the generally accepted site of the miracle of the feeding of the 5000, although we have already noted the other possible site at Bethsaida, further around the coast. As previously mentioned, this beautifully situated church has a sixth-century mosaic below its altar. There has been a church on this site since AD350, making it one of the first sites relating to Jesus to be identified.

Taking the five loaves and the two fish and looking up to heaven, he gave thanks and broke them. Then he gave them to the disciples to distribute to the people. They all ate and were satisfied, and the disciples picked up twelve basketfuls of broken pieces that were left over.
LUKE 9:16–17

Further along the shoreline is St Peter's Church—another small but beautifully located site, right on the lake. It's a good spot for sitting and reading with the lake before you, or for paddling (or more) in the water. Inside the church is an ancient rock which may have been the place where Jesus and the disciples rested and prepared breakfast, and where Jesus appeared to the disciples for the third time after his resurrection:

Jesus said to them, 'Bring some of the fish you have just caught.' So Simon Peter climbed back into the boat and dragged the net

*ashore. It was full of large fish, 153, but even with so many the
net was not torn. Jesus said to them, 'Come and have breakfast.'
None of the disciples dared ask him, 'Who are you?' They knew
it was the Lord. Jesus came, took the bread and gave it to them,
and did the same with the fish. This was now the third time Jesus
appeared to his disciples after he was raised from the dead.*

JOHN 21:10–14

Both churches are open every day until 5.30 pm unless
there are services on—for example, on Sundays. Services
are normally taken in a range of languages, so look on the
noticeboards for services in English: if you're lucky, you may
catch one when you visit.

Capernaum

Down on the shores of the lake, only 20 minutes by road
out of Tiberias, are the remains of Roman Capernaum. A
huge site, only part of it has been excavated and it would
have been home to perhaps 2000 people at the time of
Jesus. Mentioned no fewer than 18 times in the Gospels,
Capernaum was undoubtedly a central location in Jesus' life
and ministry. It is where he called his first disciples—local
fishermen—to follow him, preached in the synagogue (the
ruins of which still remain) and healed the sick. Today there
is a beautiful modernist church built above the site of Peter's
house, a house which was an important meeting place for
Jesus and the disciples in those early days.

Allow at least an hour or two for your visit here. Entrance
costs 3–10 NIS, depending on the amount of excavation
work disrupting the site. There's a small gift shop that also
sells refreshments at the ticket booth, plus another on the

other side of the car park. If you've driven, you can continue around the shores of the lake or double back to Tiberias. Note that there are few facilities, shops or garages if you continue around the Sea of Galilee.

Footsteps

There's a moment, as you walk through the Roman ruins of the town of Capernaum, when the historical reality of what you're doing can actually dawn on you. Among the great white columns of the first-century synagogue and alongside the Herodian town walls shading you from the intense heat of the sun, you can find yourself literally following in the footsteps of Jesus.

This is exactly where the man walked, preached, lived among his disciples, performed miracles, fished with James and John and acted out his ministry. To be among the buildings, on the dusty streets where Jesus trod and at the shores of the lake where he fished is a moving experience for many, and a very important one for us as Christians. Standing at the Sea of Galilee is the closest we can get to sharing his specific time and place. It's a very different feeling to the one that greets you in Rome or even Jerusalem. What you get around the lake is a very strong sense of Jesus the man— someone just like you and me, who lived and breathed, walked and talked, loved and despaired among the villages of the Galilee 2000 years ago.

Unlike other religions, Christianity has no central doctrine of pilgrimage or homage to the Holy Land. People do go on pilgrimage, but they are a tiny fraction of the two billion Christians around the world. Yet here in the Holy Land we can get cheek by jowl to the characters and locations of the New Testament. Whether you are visiting the site of the first miracles, the scene of the annunciation or the location of the Beatitudes, Galilee opens your eyes to the events that began as a domestic Jewish drama but turned into a movement that would change the world. Reading about that domestic Jewish drama while standing or sitting in the places where it happened is not just affirming for your faith but affirming for your humanity, too—for the life of Jesus was, among other things, just another human life, and what we know about it is surprisingly little. We know nothing about his activities for most of his 33 years on this earth. The Gospels only really take up the story once his ministry starts. But what we do know about his ministry, we also know, took place in this very area, and that makes any visit exciting and rewarding.

Late in the day, as the sun sets like a pearl upon the water of the lake, shrouding the land in a hundred shades of pink, we can watch the fishermen returning to the harbour at Tiberias in their wooden boats and imagine Jesus doing exactly the same. There's plenty to see and do on the water, on the roads and via the pathways, but perhaps most importantly, this region is the only place in the world where Christians can get to grips with the undoubted locations of Jesus' ministry. For that reason alone, Galilee deserves to be at the very top of your Holy Land itinerary.

The Church of the Beatitudes

Just a mile or so up on the hill above Capernaum, with a stunning view over the Sea of Galilee, stands the site of the Sermon on the Mount. From this spot, and starting with his blessings, or Beatitudes, Jesus set out a radical message regarding who would enter the kingdom of heaven and why:

Now when Jesus saw the crowds, he went up on a mountainside and sat down. His disciples came to him, and he began to teach them. He said: 'Blessed are the poor in spirit, for theirs is the kingdom of heaven.'

MATTHEW 5:1–3

As one of his first recorded sets of teachings, the Sermon on the Mount was a remarkable first move, and the site today is an inspiring spot overlooking the water. Tiberias is visible in the distance, as are the high hills on either side of the lake.

Footsteps

The Beatitudes are among the most famous lessons from the Gospels. Despite their simplicity and consistency with the rest of Jesus' message, the Beatitudes are a remarkably radical declaration of a new covenant between the Jews and their God. They are a clear demonstration of how Jesus was challenging the status quo of the time as he sought to push thoughts and motives in contrast to traditional Jewish teaching.

Built on one of the purported sites of the Sermon on the Mount, today's church is barely 100 years old. The architect was Antonio Barluzzi, who was also responsible for the Church of the Annunciation in Nazareth and the Church of the Transfiguration at the summit of Mount Tabor (see pages 146–48 for more details of his work). The octagonal form was inspired by Jesus' eight blessings and there is a study centre, accommodation and a gift shop as well as the church itself. Allow an hour to walk through the buildings and lush gardens, with their themed stone monuments and perfectly manicured lawns.

Zefat

A further 20 miles north of the Sea of Galilee is the buzzing hilltop town of Zefat, or Safed. Famed as the birthplace of Kabalah, Zefat played a key part in the Israeli war of independence, when the local Arab population was driven from the town by a mere handful of Jewish fighters with a notoriously misfiring mortar cannon, the Davidka mortar.

As well as the connection with Kabalah, the town and its location have inspired an important artists' colony. There are dozens of art galleries clinging to the hillside below Davidka Square, where many single-artist shops are run and staffed by the painters themselves.

If you want to stay the night, check out the Safed Inn, a 20-minute walk from the centre, which charges around £50 per night for a double room and has a superb breakfast selection as well as a jacuzzi and plenty of chill-out space. It is popular with independent travellers, and the owners can give sound advice on what to see in and around town.

Tel Dan and Banias

These National Park sites are in the far north of the Golan, beyond the town of Kiryat Shmona (which has some good cafés and supermarkets, should you need to stock up). They are both on the Lebanese border and are surrounded by uncleared landmine fields. You should steer clear of anywhere fenced off by barbed wire or with a 'danger' sign.

Tel Dan reveals one of the sources of the Jordan as it tumbles downhill from the crags above, while at Banias a second of the Jordan's springs forms a beautiful waterfall. The walks are sublime and feel a world away from the dusty heat of the Galilee. It's not quite a mini-Switzerland up here, but the scenery and walks are among the best in Israel.

Both sites are open every day until 5.30 pm, with last admissions an hour before that. Entry at each is 25 NIS.

Nimrod Castle

The most atmospheric Crusader castle in Israel, Nimrod Castle is another National Park site worthy of the drive north. A good hour and a half from Tiberias, this region is also much cooler and greener than anything further south. It's a beautiful corner of Israel and the ruins of the castle itself jut out from the mountainside on a perfect, narrow promontory, seemingly immune from attack. Even the drive up makes you gawp in wonder, while clambering over the ruins makes you wonder how the stonework for the castle was ever constructed in such a precarious setting.

Actually built by the Muslim armies (led by Al-Aziz Uthman, nephew of Saladin) to protect the trade routes to Damascus, the castle was regularly besieged by the Crusaders. It had fallen into ruin by the 16th century and was used as a prison for a while by the Ottoman Turks. The 25 NIS entry fee is payable at a ticket office in the car park, next to a small café with tremendous views. In the far distance on a clear day, the Sea of Galilee is visible, although it's often too hazy here to see further than a few miles. Even the valleys below look far away.

Mount Hermon and the Golan Heights

The villages clinging to the slopes of Mount Hermon are small and focus mainly on providing ski services to Israelis coming up to ski in winter or hike in summer. Majdal Shams is the only settlement of any size and it only holds a few hundred families. In winter, this is the place where everyone heading up the mountain to ski prefers to eat, drink and sleep, so it can become unbearably crowded. The village does allow access to the ski field about five miles above town and higher on the western slopes of Hermon itself. The ski resort bottom car park also allows access to the miles of hiking trail, which can be accessed at any time of year unless there is deep snow.

The highest point on the Israeli side of the mountain reaches 2236 metres; the summit slightly above and beyond this is on the Syrian side of the border and reaches 2814 metres. The summit zone is a riot of wild flowers from April until July, by which time the snow has usually melted away completely. You can access the ski lifts all year round, since they help to bring hikers and wildlife enthusiasts up to the summit. Prices vary, but expect to pay around 50 NIS for a return trip on any of the five chair lifts in the ski area. You can, of course, hike for free if you'd prefer, but even a short round trip from the skiing area car park to the summit will take between three and four hours.

Consult www.hermonski.co.il for year-round weather reports before you drive up.

Further reading

Paul Lawrence, *The Lion Concise Atlas of Bible History* (Lion Hudson, 2012).

–Chapter 8–

The Mediterranean coast

A guide to Akko, Caesarea, Haifa and Tel Aviv. These are all historically important locations with a fascinating mixture of Crusader, Roman and modern history.

- ❖ Rosh HaNikra
- ❖ Akko
- ❖ Haifa
- ❖ Mount Carmel and the Carmelites
- ❖ Caesarea
- ❖ Megiddo
- ❖ Tel Aviv

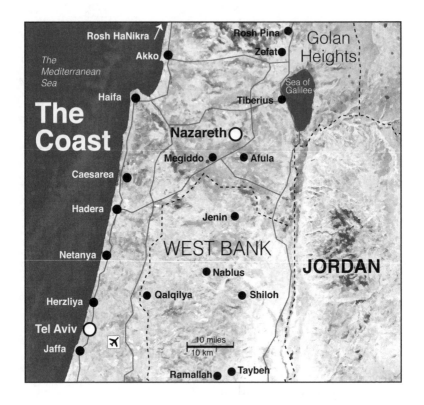

Rosh HaNikra

Moving from north to south, the coastal strip of Israel offers much of interest. Starting at Rosh HaNikra, the chalk and limestone sea cliffs are well worth an hour's visit, to walk the damp tunnels that weave around the sea and to view the Lebanese border at (very) close quarters. Often forming part of organised day tours of Akko, it's also easy to drive up here yourself, but be aware of heavy traffic on the main coast road (Highway 4) on the sabbath and public holidays.

A cable car runs down to the foot of the cliffs (30 NIS, including entry fee) or you can paddle your way round to the site from the nearby holiday village, which has nice cabins on the beach from around £40 per night. Paddle boards, sailboards and surf boards can be rented from 30 NIS, and private lessons (in English) can be accessed for around 200 NIS per hour. All of these activities and more are advertised at the holiday village office and neighbouring café.

Footsteps

Jesus almost certainly spent time around the Mediterranean during his 33 years. The Galilee, like anywhere in Israel, is not far from the coast and the main trade routes would have led to the sea ports. Akko in the north of Israel is easily accessible today from both Tel Aviv and Galilee and is a great historical destination in its own right. It was an important port city during Jesus' time and was the capital of the Crusader kingdom, which stood for 200 years before the Crusaders were defeated by Saladin and his army at the Horns of Hattin near Tiberias in 1187.

Today, a few days on the coast can come as a pleasant relief from the heat of the interior, even though it's not always on the pilgrim's itinerary. There's some great food to be had, especially seafood, and watersports to participate in, particularly surfing and windsurfing at many of the beaches between Haifa and Hadera. Check out Shonit, Sdot Yam and Arubot beaches, north and south of Caesarea, if you want to catch a few waves. Another pull of the coast is the benign Mediterranean water and the opportunity to swim safely at many of the public beaches, especially in Tel Aviv. Israel may not be the classic sun, sea and sand destination, but if that is what you want,

you'll find it in abundance up and down the coastal strip from Tel
Aviv to Haifa.

Rosh HaNikra also presents a chance to see the Israel–
Lebanon border up close. At almost the exact spot where the
cable car runs down the pure white cliffs to the sea, the road
comes to an abrupt halt. The Lebanese border is just a few
dozen metres away. At the foot of the dramatic cliffs, you can
walk through the abandoned tunnels of the coastal railway
that once ran from Tel Aviv all the way to Beirut. Could
anyone ever see this line reopening? It's a fanciful notion
but not as daft as it first sounds: Israel Railways is currently
formalising plans to open a new line through the Negev and
into Jordan to link to the coast—an idea that, 30 or 40 years
ago, would have been laughed out of the room.

Akko

Nowhere does the Crusader history of the Holy Land come to
such vivid life as it does in Acre—or Akko, as it's pronounced
in Hebrew. This honey-coloured stone city has survived
remarkably intact over the centuries and the Old City here
is one of Israel's finest medieval monuments. It is a network
of alleyways, underground catacombs, tunnels, ramparts and
ancient houses still in residential use today by the city's Arab
population.

Just as in Jerusalem, the very fabric of this port city
breathes history. Key locations around the Old City include
the tunnels, citadel and prison museum. The Al-Jazzar
mosque is one of the oldest along the coast and is close to the

packed souq and neighbourhood restaurants, which serve up a standard mix of salads and breads with hummus, grilled meats and fish. The very best eating options, however, are at the places along the rampart walls looking out to sea where you can eat seafood caught that day as the sun sinks in hues of red, pink and gold into the calm waters of the Med. In the evening, the city really comes into its own, with a peaceful but lively vibe—part family, part nightlife—as the cafés crank up the atmosphere. This is a great place to get the hang of smoking a sheesha pipe if that's your thing!

A scramble along the city walls will bring you eventually to the lighthouse that marks the far south-western corner of the city's once much larger harbour. At one time, this port saw hundreds of ships anchor and discharge cargoes of Crusader soldiers from every corner of Europe. It was mainly the English, French and Germans who convened here to spend nearly 200 years battling the forces of Saladin and his successors over control of Jerusalem and the surrounding country. Those epic wars of religion still fascinate people today, and it's worth getting to grips with your Crusader history before arriving, in order to get the most out of what's on offer.

An extended stay can be rewarding, with the chance to soak up the atmosphere of this unique city at different times of the day and night. A walk through the alleyways and along the ramparts after dark is a very different experience from a mid-afternoon stroll, when you will be just another of the many thousands of tourists who descend on the place every lunchtime and afternoon. Very few take the trouble to stay the night, despite some very good and affordable accommodation options, including the budget-priced Walleed's Akko Gate Hotel and Hostel on Saladin Street, close to the central market. The well-equipped and almost brand new official HI (Hostelling International) youth hostel at the gate through the city walls on Weizmann Street is excellent value and has great rooms of all types—dormitories, twins and doubles. This is also one of the best options for families, who can take a four- or six-bed ensuite room for themselves. There are some standard and luxury-priced hotel options in the new part of the city: the Palm Beach Club is best and allows access to a superb beach overlooking the Old City in the distance.

Transport links via Haifa are excellent and Akko is also a springboard for both the road and the rail links further north, most notably to Rosh HaNikra. If you are driving, Akko is an easy day trip from the Galilee or even from further south, although it's best to park in the new town and walk in than try to get through the city walls into the Old City itself.

Haifa

A contradictory city, this centre of Israel's heavy industries and major port is also a beautiful place, with the stunning Baha'i gardens at its heart. Haifa feels quite different from anywhere else in Israel. At times more industrial and more European, the city is also a beacon for multiculturalism and demonstrates how dangerous it is to stereotype any part of this region. Haifa proves that Jews and Muslim Arabs—as well as Arab Christians, the Baha'i and many other sects and minorities—can live together. The fact that this reality is not headline-grabbing enough means that Haifa is seldom in the news.

Practically, the best way to understand Haifa is to view it from Mount Carmel (Carmel Centre is the true city centre, with a high concentration of shops and offices) and work your way down from there. Leading down to the German Colony, with its designer stores and pavement cafés, the 19 tiered terraces of the Baha'i gardens are the most holy site to followers of the Baha'i faith and also present a beautiful view of perfectly manicured lawns.

Footsteps

In 1850, when the Persian spiritual leader Al-Bab was persecuted for his beliefs, imprisoned by the authorities and eventually executed by firing squad, his followers began planning how to continue his teachings. One of his disciples, Mirza Hussein Ali, having declared himself Baha'u'llah, was driven out of Persia and imprisoned in Baghdad and then Akko, where he died. This happened after he had spent several years recording the tenets of a new faith, based on the Abrahamic traditions but with a universal code of unity, peace and equality with all humanity. It became the Baha'i faith, which today has five million followers worldwide. The association with Mount Carmel comes from Baha'u'llah's visits, when he declared that Al-Bab's remains would one day be interred upon the mountain. The Tomb of the Bab in the very heart of the gardens is the fulfilment of this wish.

The daily tours of the Baha'i World Centre (which operate at midday, every day except Wednesday, on a first-come, first-served basis, so aim to get there early) reveal this history and more as you walk up through the stunning 19 tiers of garden. As Christians we should be able to identify with the persecution of Al-Bab and his followers, his execution and his subsequent burial here on Mount Carmel. Now the headquarters of the entire faith, the complex contains administrative buildings as well as a visitors' centre and is as peaceful as it is beautiful. For more information on the Baha'i faith and Mount Carmel, consult www.bahai.org.

> *Throughout history, God has revealed Himself to humanity through a series of divine Messengers, whose teachings guide and educate us and provide the basis for the advancement of human society. These Messengers have included Abraham, Krishna, Zoroaster, Moses, Buddha, Jesus, and Muhammad. Their religions come from the same Source and are in essence successive chapters of one religion from God. Bahá'u'lláh, the latest of these Messengers, brought new spiritual and social teachings for our time. His essential message is of unity. He taught the oneness of God, the oneness of the human family, and the oneness of religion.*
>
> <small>FROM THE BAHA'I WEBSITE: WWW.BAHAI.ORG</small>

For Christians, it is interesting to see the recurrent themes of sacrifice and unity following through into other faiths, such as the Baha'i. Jesus' message and example found resonance not just in first-century Palestine: they have echoed down the ages and inspired many other religious people, including non-Christians.

Haifa's city centre feels at times European, at times almost North American. Perched on a hill, San Francisco style, the downtown area allows constant glimpses of the sea and the steep streets of the city leading down to it from all directions. An abundance of shops and top-quality cafés and restaurants contributes to the exceptionally laidback atmosphere on streets like Hanassi Avenue and Ye'fe Not Street. Excellent places to eat include The Olive and Hamimi. Staying in the city is not quite as expensive as it is in Tel Aviv or Jerusalem, with the best budget option being the Port Inn guesthouse (down near the port), which gets consistently good reviews. Double rooms there cost from £40 per night. Standard options include the Beth Shalom guesthouse (run by the Lutheran Church) on Hanassi Avenue, which has clean, simple rooms and a lovely library with views. The luxury hotels tend to be along the top of the hill, where the likes of the Villa Carmel and the Nof Hotel cost around £150 per night. These city centre hotels are expensive, but your money will buy you some stunning views.

Most trains and buses run from the Hof HaCarmel stations to the rest of Israel. Haifa is also an essential part of the route north along the coast and east towards the Galilee, although for routes east and north the bus station at Lev HaMifratz is the main hub, not the one at Hof HaCarmel, and will feature inevitably on any attempt to see the wider region by public transport. As in the rest of Israel, the bus infrastructure is excellent, with low prices and frequent services even to smaller places like Beit She'an and Megiddo. Continuing north and east by car is also easy, with all of the principal car hire firms present in the city. Eldan often has the best rates, or, if you have time, you can call in person at the car hire offices centred around Lev HaMifratz and see if you can haggle an even better deal than is offered on the web. Beware some fairly tight parking controls in the city itself, however.

Mount Carmel and the Carmelites

The heart of Haifa is, of course, the streets that descend the hill from Carmel Centre. Mount Carmel represents the tail-end (or start!) of a longer ridge, which is mentioned in the

Bible. The point where the ridge meets the sea is also the point at which third-century locals built a small town and then a port, often Arab-dominated, which in the 20th century became the thriving commercial Israeli city that it is today.

To the east of the city centre is the most important of the Carmelite shrines. This Catholic Christian sect, founded by Crusaders seeking a contemplative life in the twelfth century, still has many bases along Mount Carmel itself, and the Monastery of St Elijah is the most important. Here the Carmelites remember the showdown with the 450 pagan prophets of Baal, as commemorated in the first book of Kings:

Then Elijah commanded them, "Seize the prophets of Baal. Don't let anyone get away!" They seized them, and Elijah had them brought down to the Kishon Valley and slaughtered there.

1 KINGS 18:40

The Carmelites' influence has ebbed and flowed throughout history, resulting in them gaining and then losing their numbers before regaining strength once more. In more recent times, their decision to aid Napoleon on his incursion into the Ottoman-controlled Holy Land led to their being removed from their shrines and monasteries by the subsequently victorious Ottomans, only returning in the 19th and 20th centuries.

Back in town, the Stella Maris Carmelite Monastery of St Elijah sits just above the Maritime Museum and Elijah's cave. Don't be surprised to see adherents of all three Abrahamic religions paying tribute to Elijah here: he is recognised as an important prophet and saint in all three faiths and, although his cave is now mainly a Jewish shrine, until 1948 it was the site of a mosque built in his honour.

Caesarea

The remains of Herod's Roman-era city reveal a place of leisure as well as trade. Getting to the site can be difficult without a hire car, so consider that option or take an organised tour from Tel Aviv, Haifa or Jerusalem. If travelling independently, the best way is to catch the train from either the north or south of the country to Binyamina station, about two miles from the site, and take a taxi for the remainder of the way. As a National Park, the site charges a 33 NIS entry fee. There is an introductory film in English and then it's easy to guide yourself around the site. Unmissable locations include the amphitheatre, the hippodrome and the Pilate stone. This large limestone block was discovered in 1960 and includes the only inscription referring to Pontius Pilate ever found. It describes him as the Roman prefect of Judea and has been dated to between AD26 and 36.

For centuries, Caesarea was one of the greatest ports in the world, with a huge retaining sea wall and harbour that made Herod's Judea one of the most prosperous regions of the entire Roman empire. There are plenty of excavated columns and stumps of sea walls to see, and the site is easily worth a couple of hours of your time. From the main entrance (one kilometre south, at the far end of the beach, is the dedicated entrance for tour groups), the first part of Caesarea is the Crusader-era citadel, which gives way to the manicured lawns in front of a row of more modern buildings. The most easily identifiable of these buildings is a 19th-century mosque constructed by the Turks. Beyond is the area where the site's maritime past comes to life, with the hugely impressive original Herodian amphitheatre and bathhouse, which has excellent mosaics.

Standing on the shore of the sea and taking in the extent of the hippodrome reminds you of the huge effort made by the Romans for public entertainment and exhibition. No right-minded citizen of the empire would miss the many chariot races, duels and other sports that occupied the amphitheatre most weeks. With a tiered 10,000-seat outdoor auditorium and room for many more standing spectators, the venue would have been important not just for the local population but also for soldiers and civil servants from the surrounding provinces.

Residents of nearby Kibbutz Sdot Yam were originally responsible for alerting the authorities to the site, and a visit to their archaeological museum is an informative way to find out more about the recent history of Caesarea, its 19th-century Serbian inhabitants and the local fishermen and farmers who began to turn up pieces of pottery 100 years ago.

There is a rather nondescript hotel nearby, belonging to the Dan chain, and a much cheaper and more hospitable B&B called Grushka (especially good for single travellers and families), slightly further away in the suburbs of Binyamina. The Grushka comes in at around £50 per night for a double room. To reach it from Binyamina railway station, walk towards town: you'll find it on HaMeyasdim Street, just one block right (east) of the main street.

North–south trains between Tel Aviv and Haifa will stop at Binyamina, where it will be necessary to pick up a taxi or hike a good two miles west towards the coast before hitting Caesarea. Equally, you can take the bus or train to Hadera and then catch the local No. 76, which runs every two hours out to Caesarea.

Megiddo

Megiddo—or Armageddon—has received a bad press over the years, but this fascinating archaeological site, known in ancient times as Chariot City, is just 20 miles inland from the coast and is easily accessible along the main Haifa–Jenin Route 66. Again, a hire car is your easiest transport option, although you can also catch a bus from Haifa or organise a taxi from nearby Afula (alleged home of the best falafel in the region) for around 50 NIS, plus 100 NIS per hour waiting time if you want your driver to wait around for you.

The site reveals a long history of battles and strategic alliances gone bad. While nothing apocalyptic has befallen Megiddo yet, John did predict that the final battle between Christ and the forces of evil will occur at the place known as Armageddon: 'Then they gathered the kings together to the place that in Hebrew is called Armageddon' (Revelation 16:16).

The excellent museum on today's National Park site (open every day until 5.00 pm, entrance fee 27 NIS) tells the multi-layered history of this area very well. There is so much here, however, that it can be hard to get your head around the incredibly long history of the place as you walk through the ruins: there's not much left to see of what was once one of the most important commercial towns and stopping points in first the Egyptian, then the Israelite and finally the Muslim world.

If you are driving through the area, take the opportunity to call in at Beit She'arim, a fascinating ancient city that was also strategically vital when the main east–west roads traversed this corner of the country. At some point in the second or third centuries AD, the site started to become a major Jewish necropolis, with many thousands being buried here. The many tombs carry inscriptions in a variety of languages—Hebrew, Greek, Aramaic and Palmyran, an ancient language related to Aramaic and used in central Syria at the time of Jesus. A walk through the underground catacombs is a chilly experience but does offer some genuine relief from the hot sun. The site is open every day until 3.00 pm, 20 NIS entry fee.

Tel Aviv

Israel's biggest city is renowned for its relaxed lifestyle, modern industries and laid-back, easygoing vibe. A modern, secular city with great beaches along the coast, it feels completely different from Jerusalem and makes a terrific contrast to the holy city. You will see few Orthodox communities here and almost no religious monuments at all: Tel Aviv has always very deliberately portrayed itself as a Western-styled liberal and open place where the faultlines of Israel's political, religious and cultural differences can seem to be kept firmly below the surface.

Tel Aviv barely existed before 1920, and for that reason alone the city we see today is, in many ways, the antithesis of ancient, religious Jerusalem. It's a fun-loving and fashionable place, packed with young people, families and professionals going about their lives, sometimes oblivious to events in the wider region. The original villages of the interwar settlement among the sand dunes have turned into a large urban sprawl with a population approaching two million. Officially merged with the nearby port city of Jaffa in 1950, Tel Aviv is logically laid out on a grid system, with the main part of the city bordered by Jaffa in the south, the Yarkon River to the north, the Ayalon Highway to the east and the Mediterranean to the west. This is a large area, though, and it can be best to focus on the axis between Yitzhak Rabin Square and the intersection of Allenby and King George Streets, which is where most of the action takes place. These streets, along with Dizengoff Square and the Carmel market, are the real heart of the city's shopping, nightlife and restaurant scene, with most of the hotels also close to this central zone.

From a practical point of view, the sights are interesting rather than mindblowing, and one major drawback of the city is that it's not cheap, especially for accommodation. There are many top-end hotels, especially on the beachfront, but fewer budget choices. Public buses and cafés can be reasonably good value for money, but hotels are often out-rageously priced even by Western standards. However, a stay of a few days—or even longer if you have time—is essential and will allow you some holiday time, especially if you simply want to eat good food, relax on the beach and enjoy the winter sunshine. The city's Bauhaus architecture and excellent galleries will give design buffs an exciting few days. You will want to see the beautiful white marble edifice of Habima Square's National Theatre and the Bauhaus arcade close to Dizengoff Square, on the way to the stunning Museum of Art on the eastern side of the city centre.

History junkies can walk the paved square in front of City Hall and think about what might have been, had Yitzhak Rabin not been assassinated here in 1995. Then check in at Independence Hall, the site of the signing of Israel's declara-tion of independence, located on historic Rothschild Boule-vard, and finish off with a walk around Ottoman-era Jaffa, with its countless flea markets and chic coffee houses. Jaffa itself can be a slightly less frenetic option than downtown Tel Aviv. The Old Jaffa Hostel (www.telaviv-hostel.com), next to the markets, is a popular choice at just £10 per night for a dormitory bed, or less for a mattress on the roof in summer, while couples or a group of four should seriously consider investing in the über-cool Andromeda apartments, up the hill to the south of the port, which come in at £150 per night (www.andromeda.co.il).

Tel Aviv nightlife is undoubtedly the best in the Middle East, with plenty of friendly bars and clubs open late into the night, including at weekends. Israelis can be incredibly friendly and hospitable and a night out even by yourself can easily end with new friendships forged and contacts made. Many people will jump at the chance to practise their English on you and it can be an ideal way to come into contact with the ordinary people whom you can easily miss when travelling through the tourist hotspots in the rest of the country. Tel Aviv forces you out of any tourist bubble that may be in place for other periods of your trip and gets you under the skin of life in modern Israel. Sitting in a café or bar or even on the beach, it is remarkably easy to make friends with the city's people, whose take on politics and life will be more varied and interesting than anything you hear from a guide or read in a book.

At the same time as being laid-back, Tel Aviv is renowned for modern problems like terrible traffic, occasional pea-soup summer smog and crazy driving. You should take care crossing the roads, but in other respects the city feels, and is, very safe. A late-night walk along the seafront promenade will see you joining many hundreds, if not thousands, of Tel Aviv residents doing exactly the same, even into the early hours of the morning. With lots of forceful architecture and an equally forceful sun for most of the year, Tel Aviv is not everyone's cup of tea, but it is a great place to relax for a few days at the end of a pilgrimage and has the reputation of being the only city in the entire Middle East where lone women can feel safe 24 hours a day.

Footsteps

My first ever stopover in Tel Aviv got off to an interesting start. As I unrolled my sleeping bag and prepared for a cheap night on the roof of the Old Jaffa Hostel, I got talking with my immediate neighbours— an English woman and a Canadian man. Like me, they were keen to sleep on the roof to get some fresh air rather than being stuck in the stuffy dorms below. It was autumn and the temperature was still in the high 30s. The couple had been travelling around Israel for some weeks while the man conducted research for a writing project.

'Oh, that's interesting, because I write as well,' I said.

Then it dawned on me. I actually recognised the man from the dust cover of one of that decade's bestselling novels, and I knew enough from that book to remember that the author was Canadian. As he went off to have a shower, I said to his companion, 'Is that Yann Martel?' She nodded and when they later invited me to join them for dinner and then for a day out the next day, I eagerly accepted.

One thing I've learnt and always rejoiced in is the truth that being on the road really does open you up to new experiences, truths and contacts. Hearing from one of the world's foremost writers on his interpretation of the history of Israel and its recent past made me feel incredibly lucky. This was a man I could learn from, with his insights into not just literature and philosophy but also religion, science and travel. It was while he was spending a year backpacking around India that he had come up with the story told in his book *Life of Pi*.

The following day we spent hours travelling round Tel Aviv while Yann had meetings with his Israeli publishers and the local media and, eventually, a reception at the Canadian ambassador's official residence. Dressed in scruffy jeans and a T-shirt, I felt very much out of place as bow-tied waiters walked round the marble-finished house with plates of canapés and trays of champagne flutes. Around the pool at the back of the house, a well-known Israeli TV presenter and his crew cornered me and asked fervently, 'So, you are Yann's friend! Tell us all about him.' They looked at me very oddly indeed when I explained I had only known him since the previous evening.

You never know whom you may meet when on the road, and this has never failed to be true for me in decades of travelling. It is one of the joys of backpacking as a youngster and travelling for work when older. As long as you remain open to what the road throws at you and are willing to take a chance on talking to strangers or joining your neighbours for dinner when asked, sometimes the world will repay your adventure with opportunities you never imagined.

Accommodation options for downtown Tel Aviv include the budget Sky Hostel or Florentine Backpackers, which have both dorms and private en-suite options at good rates. Ben Yehuda and Sea Land apartments offer spacious self-catering rooms and are both close to Hilton Beach. Each offers good value at around £50 per night. At the luxury end, try the international-standard Sheraton or Crowne Plaza, both on the seafront, or, for a bit more local character, go for the Alma Hotel further into town, all at around £140 per night.

Further reading

Peter Walker, *The Story of the Holy Land: A visual history* (Lion Hudson, 2013).

–Chapter 9–

Beyond Israel and Palestine

A look at the Sinai peninsula in Egypt and relevant sites in nearby Jordan.

❖ Introduction
❖ Egypt
❖ St Catherine's Monastery and Mount Sinai
❖ Sinai coast
❖ Jordan
❖ Jordan Valley
❖ Petra
❖ Aqaba and Wadi Rum
❖ Travel details

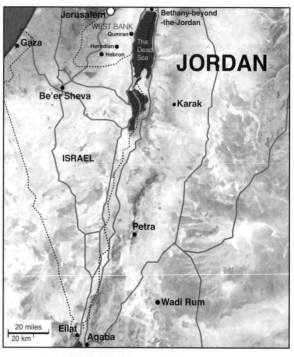

Introduction

From Israel it's well worth taking the opportunity to visit Egypt and Jordan if you have time.

Eilat, on the southernmost tip of Israel, makes a good access point with relatively hassle-free border crossings and short travel times to the major sights in the neighbouring cities. The Allenby Bridge crossing into Jordan—just past Jericho—is, however, a better access point if you want to catch Mount Hebo and Bethany Beyond the Jordan, the most likely location of Jesus' baptism by John the Baptist. Amman also makes a good base for checking out these sights before heading further south in Jordan to take in Petra. You could then re-enter Israel for a round trip: Jerusalem to Amman, Amman to Petra, Petra to Aqaba and then Eilat can easily be done in a couple of days, although spending four or five days will bring greater rewards.

Despite having no biblical connections that we know of, the obvious next destination after upper Jordan is Petra, which is simply a must for anyone visiting the region. Add Mount Sinai in Egypt and both become feasible in a few days each if travelling overland, or in a week if joined together in a round trip. Independent travellers may be nervous because of recent security concerns in Egypt, but, at the time of writing, travel in the region is still largely safe. Keeping an eye on the latest news and reading internet forums about the places you wish to visit can offer reassurance if you are having doubts. You can also ask questions of other travellers if you are still concerned about safety in the region. Above all else, as long as it's safe, Sinai is well worth the effort and can be reached from Jordan or Eilat, or by flying into Sharm el-Sheikh on the southern tip of the Sinai coast, direct from the UK.

There are, of course, many further biblical sites around the Mediterranean and Middle East that fall outside the scope of this guide, and the same is true with regard to some of Israel's other neighbours. While it is not impossible to visit the Gaza Strip or Lebanon, it is not recommended or easily attempted from Israel. There is no open border crossing between Israel and Lebanon, for example, so any excursion north would involve an entirely different trip routed through another country, and Gaza has seen almost a decade of instability since elections returned a Hamas government to office in 2006. There have been regular Israeli military incursions over the past few years, resulting in many thousands of deaths.

If you are adamant about getting into Gaza, however, and can arrange for a local organisation to sponsor you, it's perfectly feasible to enter at either the Erez crossing from Israel or the Rafah crossing point from Egypt. Under Egypt's Mubarak regime, the border was closed, but the Rafah point has been open for the past two years. It's worth reiterating that you will need a local sponsor inside Gaza to help you make the journey and, while the territory is probably safer than the images we see on the news would suggest, Gaza does represent an increased personal security risk and you should think twice before attempting to travel there.

Because Israel and Jordan recognise one another, an excursion to Petra or Aqaba, for example, presents no visa or entry problems for Westerners. The same goes for Egypt and a trip along Sinai's Gulf Coast to Mount Sinai, one of the oldest Christian pilgrimage sites on earth. Recent political instability in Egypt has badly affected the tourism industry and frightened many travellers away. Kidnappings by local bedouin have occurred on the Sinai peninsula but, in response, the Egyptians have launched some hefty military operations, which may make you feel more comfortable about going there. Tourism is still a major part of the Egyptian economy and the military maintains a constant presence throughout the peninsula.

We have still to see how the current insecurity in the country and wider Middle East plays out, but despite everything else going on, life at St Catherine's Monastery tends to carry on largely unaffected, just as it has for the past 2000 years. If you can (and want) to get out there, you will find one of the most inspiring pilgrimage sites anywhere, fabled for centuries not just because of the connection to Moses, but also as a place to sit quietly, reflect, pray and experience some beautiful desert landscapes.

If sitting on a mountaintop, drinking in the desert view, doesn't sound like your idea of fun, then Sinai will not be for you, but, for the more adventurous-minded, it is a feasible and desirable place to visit. Just keep a careful eye on current events and, again, once in the region, speak with fellow travellers rather than tour reps (who may be bent on selling you an excursion) or taxi drivers (who will promise the earth) before making up your mind whether to travel there or not. Trusting your own instincts is usually the best way to judge these things. Only you know how risk-averse you are, but it's worth remembering that there are risks associated with everything in life and media portrayals are not always true to the facts on the ground.

Footsteps

Catching the ferry from Aqaba in Jordan to Nuweiba in Egypt is a bit of an adventure in itself and reminded me that travel in this part of the world was difficult 2000 years ago and still can be today.

I'd heard that the ageing catamaran (complete with orange and green seats, which make you feel slightly queasy as soon as you get on board) is often late, sometimes by several hours, and fails to run at all on some days. So I was pleasantly surprised to find the vessel waiting for me at the docks at Aqaba with plenty of first-class seats available at $90 each (second class is $15 cheaper).

As I readied myself for a short sleep, I became almost completely overwhelmed by diesel fumes so decided to make a beeline for the open deck. However, as I was about to discover, being a catamaran, the vessel had no open deck. I realised it was going to be a long trip. I may not have been walking to Egypt, like Mary and Joseph with the baby Jesus, but it was still a taxing journey.

There were only another couple of Westerners on the catamaran: the majority of passengers were Egyptian workers travelling back from Jordan to their Sinai homes. Upon arrival in Nuweiba, there was a long wait (over an hour) to clear immigration and customs and I felt terribly out of place among the ordinary working people of Egypt. The usual throng of taxi drivers and people offering to carry my bag greeted me, and I walked away from the docks to wait until the initial rush had died down, before picking one of the eager drivers and negotiating a good price for the onward journey.

Egypt

Jeremy Bowen, the BBC's long-serving Middle East editor, says it all in his book on the Arab uprisings: the reason why the region is so important is that the axis of the entire Arab world hinges on Egypt. With one in four Arabs being of Egyptian descent and Cairo being the epicentre of Arabic culture, the country remains strategically vital. Now, for the very first time, its people have had the chance to articulate their views politically. If they can make a go of democracy here, it will bode well for the rest of the region. On the flip side, failure could signal something catastrophic.

The land of Egypt has always been important to the story of Jesus, and that connection has endured through the presence of the Coptic Church, headquartered in Alexandria and the oldest continuing church in the world.

> *So he got up, took the child and his mother during the night and left for Egypt, where he stayed until the death of Herod. And so was fulfilled what the Lord had said through the prophet: 'Out of Egypt I called my son.'*
> MATTHEW 2:14–15

The Coptic Christian minority in Egypt makes up as much as ten per cent of the population—more in Alexandria and the southern region around Aswan. Here we have a Christian minority who are often economically better off as well as better educated than their Muslim brothers and sisters, and yet they feel so insecure about their future that they appear intent on leaving their homeland. It can seem as if every Christian you talk to speaks about emigrating to Europe or the United States. It can be profoundly depressing to think that Egyptian Christians, with a chance to make their voice heard democratically and have their status guaranteed in law for the first time, are now getting ready to leave the land of their birth.

People will tell you that security is the only issue in Egypt right now—that, and the economy. While there is no shortage of everyday goods (if you have money, you can still buy yourself some insulation from the crisis outside) the future economy of the country looks stalled at best. Many Christians see no future for themselves or their children in fighting for their rights to coexist in harmony. Their fears are understandable. There have been ten bomb attacks against churches in Cairo alone in the past two years, resulting in over 80 deaths. While such attacks are always condemned by the government, Christians feel they are being made a scapegoat by others around them for the situation that everyone is facing. Being a member of a persecuted minority must feel horrendous, and we must try to support Egypt's Christian community as much as we can. With just 15 million Christians left in the Middle East, we need to be alive to the plight of our brothers and sisters and try to understand their conflicting desires both to remain and to leave.

Despite the recent political instability, Egypt is still an amazing place to visit and has some of the world's greatest historic sites, easily accessible through Cairo, Luxor and Aswan. With the pyramids and Egyptian Museum in Cairo worthy of a few days' visit, the Valley of the Kings near Luxor the same, and Aswan too, a three-centre week-long trip to Egypt can be enjoyed even before heading over to Sinai to experience the magic of St Catherine's and Mount Sinai. Local tours and taxis are reasonably priced and Cairo is still a largely welcoming city, which feels more relaxed than you may expect. However, try to keep away from political demonstrations and Tahrir Square (next to the Egyptian Museum).

This chapter focuses mainly on the Sinai as an add-on to a wider pilgrimage to Israel, the West Bank and Jordan. Egypt could justify a two-week visit in its own right, and, as pointed out elsewhere, a month in the region, split equally between Israel, the West Bank, Jordan and Sinai, would reward the traveller with some amazing experiences. An extended stay also allows you to begin to get 'under the skin' of what makes this part of the world tick and ensures that you don't spend all your time rushing between different cities.

Aside from the Sinai, Cairo is the obvious entry point for Egypt, as it has excellent connections through a modern airport and good transport links to the rest of the country and wider region. Return flights with airlines such as BA or EgyptAir begin at around £400, or less when they have their world sales on. Cheaper charters direct to Luxor and the Sinai or scheduled services with Easyjet are also available. EU nationals can purchase a visa upon arrival at any Egyptian airport, valid for 30 days in the first instance. Local taxis can be negotiated down to around £10 for a trip from airport to city centre, while many hotels will arrange pick-up for you if notified in advance.

Travelling first or second class on the local trains is another good option. The country's principal rail line runs from Cairo along the Nile to Luxor and on to Aswan. Tickets are available from the ticket booths at Cairo's Ramses station (take the subway under the platforms to the far side of the station) or from local travel agents. Journey times are seven hours from Cairo to Luxor and another four hours from Luxor to Aswan. There is a Nile sleeper every evening, which departs Cairo at 10.00 pm and arrives in Aswan at 11.00 am. First-class tickets cost about £30 for the entire journey.

It's perhaps stating the obvious to say that now is the time to visit Egypt if you're looking for great-value accommodation. Even high luxury at places like the five-star Kempinski Nile, Intercontinental, Grand Nile Tower or Fairmont Nile (all in superb locations) costs around £110 per night for a double or twin. Standard-price hotels include the excellent Concorde and Conrad downtown and the Sofitel or Mövenpick Pyramids resorts out at Giza. Budget options include the Cairo Moon, which has double rooms for the price of a dorm bed anywhere else in the world, and the Grand Pyramids Hotel at Giza, which is of a good international standard but also charges hostel prices—£20 per night for a single room, including breakfast and use of the swimming pool and gym.

In Luxor, try the Pavilion, Sheraton or Maritim Jolie, all at less than £50 per night. In Aswan, the Mövenpick or Sofitel resorts are a great deal and offer stunning views of the Nile and city. Local tours can be arranged to head down to Abu Simbel to see the Sun Temple and will cost around £100 for an overnight trip with food and flights—a little more expensive if you take a cruise out there from Aswan. It is well worth the expense, however, and lets you experience one of the wonders of the world. It also supports tourism in a very poor part of the country.

Along the Red Sea coast (centred on the dive resort of Hurghada, which also has direct charter and scheduled flights from the UK and the rest of Europe), there are several interesting sites to see. Travelling this way from Cairo also enables you to take an alternative trip to Cairo–Luxor–Aswan. A Cairo–Hurghada–Sharm–Sinai trip is entirely feasible using taxis, local buses and internal EgyptAir flights (to cross from Hurghada to Sharm).

For Christian pilgrims, the main draw of the Red Sea coast is the presence of the two oldest monasteries in Egypt. The coastal town of Zafarana on the Gulf of Suez is the nearest main settlement from which you may wish to take a taxi if you are not on an organised tour from Cairo. A taxi up to St Anthony's Monastery and back from the coast will cost around £20 plus waiting time. Note that all Cairo–Hurghada buses will drop you at the turn-off for St Anthony's, about 15 minutes after you've left the outskirts of Zafarana. From here it's a tough 15-kilometre uphill walk, so be prepared. Taxis can also be arranged to take you on a round trip from Cairo for around £50, or you may wish to join an organised trip from Cairo's Coptic church, which runs bus tours to both monasteries at weekends. Ask around at St Mark's Cathedral or in Old Cairo's Coptic Quarter for details.

St Anthony was one of the early Christian saints and lived the hermit life here among the Egyptian hills. He is regarded as the first ever monk. Along with his protégé St Paul (not the apostle Paul), Anthony fled persecution in Alexandria shortly after Christianity began to spread through the ancient world. Paul was so devout and so inspired by his older mentor that he too took to the hermit life from the age of 16 onwards. St Anthony's Monastery is a beautiful oasis among high red cliffs, offering a magnificent view of the coast and distant Sinai from the summit of the hill behind the monastery complex (allow an hour to hike up—best done at sunset). You will pass St Anthony's cave en route, where pilgrims ancient and modern have scrawled graffiti on to the walls and left prayers on notepaper, Wailing Wall-style, in the cracks of the cave wall. An hour spent on the summit of the ridge is a spellbinding experience.

The less-visited St Paul's Monastery is a 20-kilometre hike along the ridge of the hills to the south-east. (Do not attempt the route without a local guide and plenty of water.) Here,

Paul saw out his last days while waiting for Anthony to bring him a cloak to die in. Today the monasteries are closely linked and, over the centuries, have seen many famous Coptic monks and saints pass through their doors. Both monasteries have a number of churches and chapels within their walls, and at both you will find an English-speaking monk who is willing to show you around and go into more detail on the lives of the two saints. Both are free to enter and have small refectories where guests are welcome. You can arrange to stay overnight at them by contacting St Mark's Church, Cairo, well in advance with your travel dates: telephone +20 2 2418 8344.

St Catherine's Monastery and Mount Sinai

Pilgrims have been coming here for centuries, ever since Christian monasticism first flourished in the heart of this rocky, arid peninsula. As Rowan Williams muses in his book *Silence and Honey Cakes*, 'The desert wisdom teaches rather than preaches... The actual substance of our relationship with eternal truth and love is bound up with how we manage the proximity of [our] human neighbours.'

A sense of fleeing from the pressures and expectations of today's world is very much in step with the experience of the original monks who fled persecution and corruption in ancient Egypt and wanted the time and space to open themselves more fully to God and others. Like monasteries everywhere, St Catherine's epitomises an outward-facing worldview that places neighbourliness at the heart of all study and teaching. Instead of being cut off from the modern world, the monks learn about, pray for and stand vigil over the life that the rest of us are so busily creating. It is these values that can attract pilgrims. There are also the obvious biblical connections. Inside St Catherine's compound, at the very rear of the complex, is the site of the burning bush itself, a major constituent of the Exodus stories of Moses leading the tribes of Israel out of slavery and back to their homeland.

> *Now Moses was tending the flock of Jethro his father-in-law, the priest of Midian, and he led the flock to the far side of the wilderness and came to Horeb, the mountain of God. There the angel of the Lord appeared to him in flames of fire from within a bush. Moses saw that though the bush was on fire it did not burn up. So Moses thought, 'I will go over and see this strange sight—why the bush does not burn up.' When the Lord saw that he had gone over to look, God called to him from within the bush, 'Moses! Moses!' And Moses said, 'Here I am.' 'Do not come any closer,' God said. 'Take off your sandals, for the place where you are standing is holy ground.' Then he said, 'I am the God of your father, the God of Abraham, the God of Isaac, and the God of Jacob.' At this, Moses hid his face, because he was afraid to look at God.*

EXODUS 3:1–6

If you are travelling independently, private taxis will be at the centre of your travel plans, so it pays to invest some time and effort in negotiating the right driver (someone who has more than just a basic command of English) for the right price (no more than half of whatever price they start by quoting). As often mentioned in this book, haggling is a way of life in this part of the world, and the best way to get what you want is to be firm about your needs and how much you are willing to pay. Ultimately, drivers make their living from tourists and would much rather earn a day's money with you than sit and wait for someone else.

As a general rule, drivers should be willing to take you anywhere up and down the coast and across to St Catherine's for around £10 each way, plus more for waiting time. This will be offered whether you've thought about it or not, so try to have an itinerary in your head before you start negotiating so that both parties understand what they are letting themselves in for. If you are planning an overnight stay, book in advance and make it clear to your driver that you only need him to take you one way. He will almost certainly give you his mobile number in case you wish to hire him again for the return journey.

A public bus runs intermittently to St Catharine's: see www.bedouinbus.com for more information. This website is also a good portal for other bedouin-based tourism initiatives and links to the St Catherine's information and accommodation websites. The bus itself provides a great service for just a few pounds, but it is infrequent and unreliable at present (the bus only runs four times per week). However, if you're flexible and you're up for an adventure, check out the times on their website, turn up on time at one of the bus stops in Nuweiba or Dahab and have your fare handy. At present, the service charges £5 each way for the journey across to the mountains in a slightly bumpy and slow minivan but it's one of the great bargains of the region and will also introduce you to other travellers and locals.

To climb Mount Sinai (Jebel Musa) itself, you will need to hire a guide. Any attempt to set off without one will bring more hassle than it's worth. For around £10 you should find someone with good English to explain things to you en route. Expect to pay the same again for a camel to carry you back down, or the same to sleep on one of the mattresses on the summit. The overnight stay is worthwhile if you have the time: to wake up to a beautiful desert sunrise should be a highlight of any trip. The camel path is the more popular and easier route to the top (allow two to three hours), while the 4000 Steps of Repentance offer a more direct ascent for the fit (maximum two hours).

If you wish to hike up the higher Mount St Catherine (Jebel Katherina), hire a guide from the collection of lodges behind the monastery. Sheikh Mousa is the best person to arrange this for you: he will charge around £100 for a multi-day hiking and camping trip into the mountains, including the summit of Mount St Catherine, which is Egypt's highest peak.

Sinai coast

It was only after the 1967 Six-Day War that Israel began to develop the Sinai peninsula for international tourism, a policy that continued after Israel left the peninsula in 1982. Development continued apace throughout the 1980s and 1990s, especially in Sharm el-Sheikh, which became the primary focus of international tourism, with its busy international airport attracting charter flights from much of Western Europe and, more recently, Russia and Eastern Europe.

Of course, bedouin tribes have populated the region for centuries, but they are a marginalised minority within Egypt. The guides and drivers hired by tour operators to take you around the sites are often bedouin, especially at St Catherine's and Mount Sinai, where their traditional homes can still be found behind the tourist facilities. In the coastal resorts they are largely shunned by their Arab neighbours.

The ease of access through Sharm is the main reason why

you would come this way—unless diving is your thing, that is. Again, even five-star resorts can currently be found for around £50 per night (try the Hyatt, Hilton or Mövenpick), and good cheap food can be bought in the town's many restaurants, which cover every conceivable cuisine from Mexican to Italian, Chinese, Malay and Thai.

Dahab is a smaller and friendlier place than Sharm, with smaller hotels and fewer big resorts. Nuweiba, further up the coast and on the way to Taba and the Israeli border, is cheaper still. Taxis and public buses run between all three towns. For 4x4 desert adventures, check out providers in Nuweiba such as Centre 4 Sinai, who will be able to tailor trips for you to places like the Coloured Canyon for around £50 per day, including food and water.

Jordan

One of the most stable of the Middle East states, Jordan has been a long-term investor in its tourist infrastructure, and for good reason. It's an enchanting place with some of the most amazing sights in the world as well as some of the most beautiful scenery in the region. Tourism is the number-one contributor to the national economy, so security remains a high priority, although to date the country has had fewer problems than any of its immediate neighbours. The Arab tribes that later came together to form the Hashemite Kingdom of Jordan played a crucial role in the defeat of the Ottoman Empire during World War I, as detailed by T.E. Lawrence in his book *The Seven Pillars of Wisdom*.

As the first Arab country to recognise Israel, Jordan's government and ruling class have always been pro-Western and have so far even managed to resist calls for greater democratisation following the Arab Spring of 2011. Jordan has been ruled by the same family since 1946. Although the current king, Abdullah, has set about reforming political life in his country, it is more a benign dictatorship than a fully functioning democracy and talk of greater freedoms has yet to bear fruit.

Amman is not the most appealing of capitals at first glance, although it is an important regional city and is built upon ancient remains: the citadel and Roman theatre in downtown Amman are equally impressive. The old city's souq and narrow hillside streets are fascinating and it's easy to lose yourself with just your camera for a good few hours in the alleyways of this ancient capital. But it's outside Amman that Jordan truly reveals itself, in the natural wonders of the south (Petra and Wadi Rum being hugely impressive and well worth a visit in their own right) and in the Crusader and Roman ruins of the north, such as at Jerash.

Jordan Valley

The east bank of the River Jordan contains several key sites for Christians. Mount Nebo, from which Moses surveyed the Jordan Valley and declared that he had seen the 'promised land', is the most profound and is a great spot, not far from Amman (less than 10 Jordanian Dinar in a taxi) with an ancient monastery on a bluff overlooking the Jordan. There are few facilities out here and people come more for the view and perhaps to read from the Bible than anything else, but it is a good starting point for a longer journey along the east bank of the Jordan.

Bethany Beyond the Jordan is on the way out to the Israeli border and is a much more likely spot for the baptism of Jesus than other claimed locations, such as Yardenit at the bottom of the Galilee or Bethany on the banks of the Jordan above Galilee. There are the remains of three churches here, including a sixth-century Byzantine basilica and a later Crusader structure. Some ancient mosaics can be seen. Entry to the site (open from 8.00 am to 4.00 pm every day, entry fee 12 JD) includes a one-hour guided tour, which is more informative than the English-language brochure that is handed out.

The Crusader sites of Madaba and Karak, further inland from the Jordan, are longstanding sites of interest. The best is Karak, with its bustling old town and ruined Crusader castle (open 8.00 am to 4.00 pm every day, entry fee 1 JD). At Madaba, St George's Church marks the saint's connections with the area with a wonderful mosaic.

Petra

Often revered as one of the wonders of the world, the 'rose red' city of Petra can certainly make a good claim for being the number-one archaeological attraction of the region. A Nabatean stone city, long lost and forgotten until 200 years ago, Petra today attracts half a million people every year to its canyons, carvings and cliffs (entry fee is a hefty and unavoidable JD 50 per person). Try to plan at least a couple of days' visit in and around its unique landscape. It's a perfect place to hike by yourself and discover the nooks and crannies of its ruins away from the crowds who pack out the Treasury and clog up the Siq. Sturdy hiking boots are essential, with walks up to the monastery or Little Petra potentially taking several hours.

If you are staying over, note that, to avoid the crowds and make the most of the spectacular views (and photo opportunities), Petra is best seen either in the early morning (between 7.00 and 8.30 am) or late afternoon/early evening (4.00–7.00 pm). From around 3.00 pm onwards, the day-tripper crowds will be hiking back to catch their buses, so sometimes a well-earned lie-in and a later start to your day can pay dividends. Just ensure you either take your own packed lunch and bottles of water or be prepared to pay extortionate amounts at the stalls that line the centre of Petra and the pathway heading up to the monastery. The 'Petra By Night' sound and light show takes place at 8.30 pm daily and costs 10 JD per person.

The small town of Wadi Musa (Valley of Moses) outside Petra contains all of the local and tourist facilities, with shops, restaurants and transportation. Wadi Musa is much less a resort area than a place simply to lay your head between tours of Petra itself, and is generally deserted during the day. The best places to eat in the evening include the Red Cave, Oriental and Mystic Pizza restaurants, which will all feed you well for less than 10 JD. Ethical gifts from the local bedouin cooperatives are for sale in the Petra visitors' centre, or from any of the hotels and camps out at Little Petra.

Some of the best-rated hotels in Wadi Musa include the budget Cleopatra, the mid-range Amra Palace and the luxury Petra Moon Hotel or Mövenpick resort. All these hotels lie towards the Petra end of town or are just off the Shaheed roundabout further up the hill. If you want to be as close to Petra as possible, break the bank and stay at the Crowne Plaza or Petra Guest House (the two hotels share facilities).

There are supermarkets as well as bus stops at both ends of town (the range of bus services to and from Petra is one weak spot in Jordan's otherwise good tourist infrastructure), although taxis and organised tour buses may be more useful even to independent travellers when trying to leave town. A minibus tour to Wadi Rum on the way down to Aqaba, for example, is far preferable to heading straight for the port, unless you are in a rush. There is a daily JETT bus service to Amman at 4.00 pm and a similar service to Aqaba at 10.30 am and 3.00 pm, but these will only run if there is sufficient demand. Expect to pay around 5–6 JD each way for the bus. The main bus stop lies at the bottom of the hill behind the Petra visitors' centre, but buses will also pick up from the Shaheed roundabout further up the hill. Taxis should cost around 50 JD to Amman, and 40 JD to Wadi Rum or Aqaba. You may have to haggle hard for these prices, though.

Aqaba and Wadi Rum

Once in Jordan, travel is pretty straightforward. Organised tours ply the main north–south route regularly so it is easy to find a tour to suit your timings and budget. There is a local bus departing Aqaba bus station for Wadi Musa at 6.00 am and 12.30 pm, priced at 6 JD. If you choose to stay in Aqaba, there are a couple of mid-priced accommodation options on South Beach Road, such as the Mövenpick resort, plus larger resorts on the Red Sea coast in the direction of Israel, such as the Intercontinental and Kempinski. It's worth a walk around the friendly central market to check out restaurants such as Al-Tarboosh or Hani Ali's. There are also countless falafel and schwarma stalls selling good-value fast food, from 1 JD. Buses and taxis centre on Princess Haya Square and behind the Sharif Al-Hussein bin Ali Mosque towards the waterfront.

Wadi Rum offers a whole series of desert adventures lasting from a few hours to several days. Once past the entry post and bedouin village (entry fee to the Wadi Rum protected area is 5 JD: you will also need to hire a guide if you have travelled here independently), the canyons and sand dunes of the amazing and beautiful landscape open up before you. The land of T.E. Lawrence and scene of battles during the Arab revolt against the Ottoman Turks, this beguiling region is best explored by a Four-Wheel Drive tour over at least a half day, with a full-day or two-day itinerary enabling you to see sights such as Lawrence's spring, Kufic rock art and the awe-inspiring Umm Fruth Rock Bridge. Keep your hiking boots on so that you can clamber over the rocky terrain, but again only under the watchful eye of a local guide. Going it alone out here is not recommended, although you may spot the occasional intrepid Westerner trying their luck on foot, on horseback, or on a camel: all can be arranged back at the entrance to the protected area.

Sleeping under the stars is often a magical experience and can easily be done by staying the night at one of the campsites located at the southern end of the rock formations. Expect to pay around 30 JD per night for a 4WD tour including food, water and overnight stay in a simple bedouin-style canvas tent, with woollen blankets and an open fire to ward off the mosquitoes that seem to go mad around dusk. Trips to and through Wadi Rum are best organised from either Wadi Rum or Wadi Musa. Wadi Rum Desert Services come recommended and can arrange one-way, multi-day excursions between Amman, Petra, the King's Highway, Wadi Rum and Aqaba.

Travel details

As we have seen, accessing Egypt and Jordan from Eilat at the southern tip of Israel is the best way to explore the two neighbouring countries overland. You can fly between Tel Aviv or Amman and Cairo or Sharm el-Sheikh, but such flights will actually place you well out of the way for your end destinations if Mount Sinai is to be the focus of your visit. How you might access the region will depend partly on time and budget.

From Eilat it is easy to grab a taxi to the Jordanian border, from where taxis on the Jordanian side can take you into town (to Aqaba for onward connections) or further afield. Allow around two hours to make the journey from Taba (Egypt) to Aqaba (Jordan) via Eilat (Israel). A taxi to Petra from Aqaba, for example, will set you back around £40. A minivan for groups of four or more will cost around £60 for the same journey.

Trips into Egypt are similarly best done first by taxi to the border. Once you are on the Egyptian side, again taxi drivers will be waiting to pick you up or you can hop on a local bus to Taba or Nuweiba for around £3 (coming from the Israeli side, walk past the taxis and touts to the building around half a kilometre past the border itself: this is the local bus station). Travelling on as far as Sharm el-Sheikh will cost around another £5 on a local bus, or £30 in a taxi.

Access to St Catherine's Monastery and the Mount Sinai area can be made directly with your own taxi and is best arranged from either Sharm or Nuweiba. Do-it-yourself bus rides will be fairly inexpensive but also offer inconvenient timings, not designed for the needs of tourists. Locally organised day or multi-day trips can also be joined from most Western-class hotels and resorts, which will be happy to help arrange and book tours for you in air-conditioned minivans. At the time of writing, these tours were still operating pretty much on a daily basis, with costs ranging from about £50 for a short visit to more than £100 for an overnight stay.

Security concerns in Egypt have had a big impact on Sinai tourism, which has made the trip down the coast a more lonely experience than it once was. There appear to be fewer independent travellers heading this way at the moment, although the main resorts continue to be busy, thanks to the package holidays and cheap flights that are available from much of Europe, especially during the winter (October half-term to February half-term), which is peak season. It's cheaper to come into the region and stay during the summer but be very careful of climbing Mount Sinai in the heat: it's not something to do in the middle of a red-hot day in July unless you are used to hiking in the heat and can carry enough water (expect to drink two litres per hour on the ascent).

Wherever you are going, it is always best to talk with fellow travellers on the ground who may have just returned from your planned location, in order to get the very latest views and insights. Bear in mind that these may be influenced by a range of factors, including nationality and personal preferences, but if the consensus of other travellers and internet forums sounds positive, then at the very least you should consider visiting. You will definitely be helping to bring much-needed cash back into the region and might just find the spiritual inspiration that so many are looking for when they come here.

Eilat undoubtedly offers the cheapest excursion options into this part of Egypt, but always remember that you will need at least US $50 in cash for your visa at the border. Travelling between towns and cities can be done safely on public transport; it is organised tours to Mount Sinai in particular that have suffered recently, with general travel along the coast largely unaffected. Local buses are deemed safer, if more uncomfortable, than taxis or tourist buses. If you have the time, they are also a lot cheaper: the trip to Sharm from Taba, for example, will cost around £10 on the bus, despite being a 100-mile journey.

A range of airlines can get you into the region: BA and Royal Jordanian fly to Amman from London Heathrow, and EasyJet flies to Amman from London Luton (as well as to Sharm). There are also dozens of charter flights per week from a range of UK airports to Sharm El-Sheikh, including Birmingham, Glasgow, Manchester, Luton and Gatwick. Thomson and Thomas Cook are the main players.

Exchange rates

At the time of writing, the local currencies have been within the following ranges over the preceding two years:

- £1 = 5.5–6.0 NIS (Israeli Shekel)
- £1 = 1.05–1.25 JD (Jordanian Dinar)
- £1 = 9–12 EGP (Egyptian Pound)

Further reading

Rowan Williams, *Silence and Honey Cakes: The wisdom of the desert* (Lion Hudson, 2003).
David Praill, *Return to the Desert: Journey from Mount Hermon to Mount Sinai* (Fount, 1995).

Resources

Books about Israel, Palestine and the Holy Land

Lonely Planet Guide to Israel and Palestine (rev. edn) (Lonely Planet, 2012).

Rough Guide to Jerusalem (rev. edn) (Rough Guides, 2012).

Rough Guide to Egypt (rev. edn) (Rough Guides, 2012).

Lonely Planet Guide to Jordan (rev. edn) (Lonely Planet, 2012).

DK Jerusalem, Israel, Petra and Sinai (rev. edn) (Dorling Kindersley, 2012).

Edward Platt, *The City of Abraham* (Picador, 2012).

William Dalrymple, *From The Holy Mountain* (Flamingo, 1998).

Mark Thomas, *Extreme Rambling: Walking Israel's separation barrier. For fun* (Ebury Press, 2012).

Rowan Williams, *Silence and Honey Cakes: The wisdom of the desert* (Lion Hudson, 2003).

David Praill, *Return to the Desert: Journey from Mount Hermon to Mount Sinai* (Fount, 1995).

Paul Lawrence, *The Lion Concise Atlas of Bible History* (Lion Hudson, 2012).

Geza Vermes, *The Complete Dead Sea Scrolls in English* (Penguin, 2011).

Norman Wareham and Jill Gill, *Every Pilgrim's Guide to the Holy Land* (rev. edn) (Canterbury Press, 2011).

Anna Dintaman and David Landis, *Hiking the Jesus Trail* (2nd edn) (Village to Village Press, 2013).

Jacob Firsel, *Go to Galilee: A travel guide for Christian pilgrims* (Village to Village Press, 2011).

Peter Walker, *The Story of the Holy Land: A visual history* (Lion Hudson, 2013).

Colin Chapman, *Whose Holy City?* (Lion Hudson, 2004).

Colin Chapman, *Whose Promised Land?* (Lion Hudson, 2002).

Simon Sebag Montefiore, *Jerusalem: The biography* (Phoenix, 2012).

Yotam Ottolenghi and Sami Tamimi, *Jerusalem* (Ebury Press, 2012).

Stefan Szepesi, *Walking Palestine* (Signal, 2012).

William Whitson (trans.), *New Complete Works of Josephus* (Kregel Academic, 1999).

Geza Vermes, *Christian Beginnings: From Nazareth to Nicaea, AD30–325* (Penguin, 2013).

The Illustrated Bible (Dorling Kindersley, 2012).

Books about Jesus

Peter Walker, *In the Steps of Jesus* (Lion Hudson, 2011).

Tom Wright, *Simply Jesus* (SPCK, 2012).

Tom Wright, *The Way of the Lord* (SPCK, 2010).

Francis Spufford, *Unapologetic* (Faber & Faber, 2012).

Brian D. McLaren, *Why Did Jesus, Moses, the Buddha, and Mohammed Cross the Road?* (Hodder & Stoughton, 2009).

Kenneth E. Bailey, *Jesus Through Middle Eastern Eyes* (SPCK, 2008).

E.P. Sanders, *The Historical Figure of Jesus* (Penguin, 1993).

Nick Page, *The Longest Week* (Hodder & Stoughton, 2009).

Stephen Cottrell, *The Nail* (SPCK, 2011).

General history

Jeremy Bowen, *The Arab Uprisings* (Simon & Schuster, 2012).
Andrew Marr, *A History of the World* (Macmillan, 2012).
Martin Gilbert, *Israel: A history* (2nd edn) (Black Swan, 2008).
Martin Gilbert, *The Holocaust* (Penguin, 1989).

Films about Jesus

Jesus of Nazareth (Franco Zeffirelli, 1977)
The Passion of the Christ (Mel Gibson, 2004)
The Last Temptation of Christ (Martin Scorsese, 1988)
Jesus of Montreal (Denys Arcand, 1989)

Index

Enjoyed

this book?

Write a review–we'd love to hear what you think.
Email: reviews@brf.org.uk

Keep up to date–receive details of our new books as they happen.
Sign up for email news and select your interest groups at:
www.brfonline.org.uk/findoutmore/

Follow us on Twitter @brfonline

By post–to receive new title information by post (UK only), complete the form below and post to: BRF Mailing Lists, 15 The Chambers, Vineyard, Abingdon, Oxfordshire, OX14 3FE

Your Details
Name _____
Address_____
_____
Town/City _____ Post Code _____
Email_____

Your Interest Groups (*Please tick as appropriate)	
☐ Advent/Lent	☐ Messy Church
☐ Bible Reading & Study	☐ Pastoral
☐ Children's Books	☐ Prayer & Spirituality
☐ Discipleship	☐ Resources for Children's Church
☐ Leadership	☐ Resources for Schools

Support your local bookshop
Ask about their new title information schemes.